Managing Generation X

How to Bring Out the Best in Young Talent

By Bruce Tulgan

Merritt Publishing
A Division Of The Merritt Company
Santa Monica, California

Managing Generation X

First edition, 1995
3rd Printing
Copyright © 1995 by Bruce Tulgan

Merritt Publishing
1661 Ninth Street
Santa Monica, California 90406

For a list of other publications or for more information, please call (800) 638-7597. Outside the United States and in Alaska and Hawaii, please call (310) 450-7234.

Library of Congress Catalogue Number: 95-079498

Tulgan, Bruce
Managing Generation X
How to Bring Out the Best in Young Talent.
Includes index.
Pages: 244

ISBN: 1-56343-111-4
Printed in the United States of America.

This book is dedicated to Debby Applegate.

TABLE OF CONTENTS

Acknowledgments

To all the Xers who consented to in-depth interviews, as well as those who have offered their thoughts in focus groups and less formal discussions: Thank you for telling it like it is and thank you for teaching me so much about our generation.

For valuable advice offered at various points along the way, I want to thank: Andrew Boose, Douglas Brinkley, Stephen Fox, Judy Glockner, David Hendin, Sidney Kirkpatrick, Timothy Seldes, Peter Shepard and Robin Straus.

For your guidance, support and friendship in this process, I want to thank: Jeff Coombs, Cathy Cronin, Marc DelGreco, Evan Dobelle, Eilhys England, David Finkelstein, John Gable, Pat Gable, Frank Gorman, David ("Hack") Hackworth, Steve Katz, Jeff Katz, Pam Covington Katz, Judy Katz and the rest of the Katz family, Mark Kurber, Evelyn Letfus, Joe Livecchi, Jay Nussbaum, Carlo Rotella, The Victory Team, Dan Tritter, Tim Walter and Tom Zablocki.

Special thanks to Evan and Hack for their kind words about the book.

I want to thank Merritt Publishing and those at Merritt: My editor, Jim Walsh, who is himself a Star Xer, has done his job with the casual brilliance befitting an Xer. He has made my book better and my life easier—so I am grateful to him. I consider him a friend. Also at Merritt, I want to thank Cynthia Chaillie for making a personal commitment to the success of this book. And I am grateful to Jan King, the publisher, for believing in this project before she even met me. Finally, I want to thank Ericka Weeks for all of her hard work in the final stages.

i

Acknowledgments

I need to acknowledge my special debt to my sister Ronna Tulgan Ostheimer. Ronna was critical to the genesis of this project. She was an important influence on my thinking, a valuable sounding board, source of counsel and confidence, and my reliable expert on behavioral psychology and self-esteem issues.

Of course, nothing would be possible without my entire family—the wondrous foundation of my existence. To my brother Jim, sister Ronna, sister-in-law Terri, brother-in-law Tom; my nieces Elisa, Perry and Erin and my nephew Joey; my grandmother Gertrude; my in-laws the Applegates, Julie, Paul, Shan and Tanya; and my parents Norma and Henry: Thank you for being the greatest family in the world. I love you.

In special thanks to my parents: Your unfailing love, friendship and support have made me everything I am today.

To Debby Applegate: You were the first to believe in this project and your faith has been my greatest inspiration. You were the first to suggest this could be a book. You have been my most adamant supporter and my most insistent critic, my most powerful creative influence and my deepest source of encouragement. You were also the one to break it to me that the first draft was "very much a first draft"—and demand that I write a second. You read every word of the first draft and made detailed comments and suggestions throughout the entire text. You have been instrumental in the completion of this book. Your brilliance and wisdom are astonishing—your heart and soul spectacular. The very thought of you would make me smile in the midst of an earthquake. This book is dedicated to you because I cannot imagine having written it without you. My gratitude is endless. I love you.

INTRODUCTION:

An Xer's Perspective On Management And The Workplace

CAUGHT BETWEEN WALL STREET AND MTV

After law school and the bar exam, I went to work at a Wall Street law firm in the fall of 1992. I was struck by the fact that, with few exceptions, the more senior lawyers in the firm didn't have a clue about how to manage people my age.

They were among the finest lawyers anywhere and I had great personal affection for many of them. They just didn't know how to bring out the best in the Xers—members of the post-Baby Boom Generation X—who worked for them. This was no small issue, considering that at least 20 percent of the lawyers and many of the support staff there were under 30 years of age. (That 20 percent is a fairly uniform statistic in major law firms, not to mention most of the major companies, in America during the mid-1990s. It will only grow larger with time.)

I don't believe the senior lawyers meant to disregard their younger employees. Rather, they seemed to have a hard time interpreting our particular needs and expectations—and an even harder time admitting that managing a new generation might require letting go of traditional methods in favor of a more flexible approach. The closest they came to treating Xers as a special management concern was to dump us in the hands of Baby Boomers, who insisted on misinterpreting our behavior in terms of their own disgruntled youth.

THE ATTITUDES OF XERS AND BOOMERS ARE GALAXIES APART

Severely misunderstood by those in charge, my peers at the law firm and I suffered in unhealthy management relationships. Of course, these relationships were the most common topic of discussion over lunch. We laughed about one senior lawyer who was in the habit of summoning young associates to his office with a three-word phone call, "Get in here."

One friend was so angry about the way she was treated that she kept a journal in her top desk drawer noting the insulting remarks directed at her each day—she left for another job before too long.

Some partners expected us to assume extraordinary responsibilities with little or no training, while others kept us on a leash so tight there was no way for us to accomplish our work.

I spent three days in Dallas working on a corporate deal with a senior partner who was so unable to disentangle himself from my duties that we were actually tripping over each other in the conference room where we worked. When I was getting ready for bed in the hotel at night, I remember wondering to myself when he was going to come in and tell me how to brush my teeth.

Interactions of this sort had a profound impact on morale at the firm, affecting the quality of our work, diminishing our loyalty and commitment, and contributing to high turnover.

I was hearing similar stories from many of my peers outside the law firm as well. Whether they were in law, medicine, banking, advertising, engineering, insurance, marketing or sales—in corporate America or the non-profit sector—most of the young people with whom I spoke were unhappy in their jobs. Instead of finding room for learning, growth and personal fulfillment in their work, Xers were finding causes of insecurity and diminished self-esteem. Where Xers hoped to build safe havens in an erratic and dangerous world, they were feeling exposed to the influences of capricious managers. Seeking, in their work, opportunities to invest their only capital, creative energy, Xers were finding managers unwilling to underwrite the cultivation of Xers' careers. Feeling unwelcome in the workplace and undervalued by managers, Xers were withholding their creative energy—seeing their managers as unworthy trustees of this investment capital.

I began to wonder about the relationship between all of this discontent and the widespread claims being made about my generation in the media. Was it true what they say about Generation X?

Are Xers cynics, just whining about our jobs and not willing to pay our dues? Are we really the slackers we are made out to be in popular culture? Is it true that Xers have short attention spans and just can't concentrate long enough to succeed in the workplace? Are we too demanding of our managers? Do we expect too much from our work? Is it true that Xers cannot stand deferred gratification? Are we nihilistic?

THE STEREOTYPES DON'T HOLD UP

These questions didn't fit what I knew about the needs and expectations of people my age. Those expressing such displeasure with their jobs were not "slackers" at all. I knew them to be intelligent, creative, hard working individuals— people who had always thrived on challenge and opportunities to succeed. Not so long before, we were excelling in school together, studying late into the night or talking with excitement about our career plans. Since we matured to the 1980s media images of financial success, both fact and fiction, our imaginations were always attuned to the pursuit of livelihood.

Conditioned to practicing self-reliance by our latchkey childhoods, Xers expected to depend on our natural entrepreneurship to attain some level of security in an uncertain future. Even as we witnessed the disintegration of the 1980s opulence, Xers remained determined to achieve comfort and prosperity by using and expanding our creative talents, planning to build our portfolios of valuable knowledge and skills.

STAR XERS DEFINE THE MANAGEMENT CHALLENGE

Most of the Xers I know are powerful achievers capable of producing effective results with impressive speed—when properly motivated. What is more, the facts about today's work force reveal that millions upon millions of Xers are well educated successful young professionals doing important work in important places—I call these people Star Xers. Star Xers work in the best law firms, medical facilities, investment banks, advertising agencies, publishing houses, accounting firms, in government, politics and public service organizations, foundations, small companies and industrial giants in every field. Star Xers are the high performers, rising leaders,

4

and water-carriers of the working world, as well as the key to the future of the American economy.

If Xers are such a valuable resource, why are managers not more committed to maximizing our potential? What is it about Xers that managers don't understand? Why are so many employers mismanaging Xers? Are there Xers out there who are being managed well? Don't managers have as much to learn from success stories as they do from stories of failure? I decided that these were the best questions to frame an inquiry into the management relationships which Xers were experiencing. I also decided to continue learning about these management relationships from the perspective of the Xers being managed, rather than following the standard procedure of trying to learn about management from managers.

THE PLAN: TALK TO XERS THEMSELVES

I bought a lap-top computer and I began scheduling interviews with Star Xers experiencing management relation-ships in a wide range of fields. I started with Xers I knew and branched out through the Rolodexes of my more generous interviewees. I made a concerted effort to create an interviewee pool that was diverse in terms of gender, ethnic heritage, geography and job experience. My interviewees ranged in age from 21 to 31 (I also interviewed several cusp-Xers born between 1961 and 1963). Many of my interviewees hold advanced degrees. All of them are college graduates. Most of them have had more than one job. I promised ano-nymity to the interviewees and all of the employers they discussed in order to invite the most frank and open re-sponses possible.

My inquiry was simple: "How are you being managed?" And, "How does that affect your work?" Each interview lasted anywhere from thirty minutes to three hours. In all, the words of eighty-five of my interviewees are included in this book. Each interview was its own great lesson and the time consuming research process was the most profound learning experience of my life.

I found the collective wisdom of Xers to be astonishing. They knew what was wrong with bad managers and what was right with good ones. Though many were unhappy, very few were unable to identify the specific management practices causing their unhappiness. Even more impressive, Xers were quick to pinpoint the techniques employed by their best managers, wishing aloud that all managers could be so effective. In sharing their stories, Xers made it clear that they were not just complaining, but rather offering detailed evaluations of their managers as well as insightful assessments of different management styles and techniques, both bad and good. These Xers were eager to give their best in good management relationships. What is more, they were ready to teach managers exactly how to bring out their best. It's just that nobody had ever asked them before. Having asked them, I can now share the lessons in this book.

MANAGERS CAN USE THE LESSONS THESE XERS SHARE

Learning the lessons of *Managing Generation X* is important for managers because Xers are doing important work in important places.

In investment banks, Xers are analysts and associates and vice presidents, driving the work underpinning financial transactions with global implications. Young traders are executing deals by the minute which affect billions of dollars in assets.

Xers have a substantial presence in both law and medicine. Young associates in law firms are performing the majority of legal research and creating many of the legal documents which effectuate corporate transactions, estate planning, and litigation. Meanwhile, there is a sizable population of Xers servicing these same law firms as paralegals. Xers are the post-graduate residents delivering front line care to millions in emergency rooms all over America, while Xer health care administrators and junior executives in insurance and pharmaceutical companies attempt to manage the financial side of medicine.

In organizations of all shapes and sizes, Xers are researchers, analysts, auditors, consultants, marketing and salespeople, and business executives. Xer scientists and engineers are setting the pace for new technological developments which promise to drive the economy of the next millennium. Young officers serving in the armed services are responsible for the training and deployment of platoons, the maintenance and utilization of billion-dollar hardware, as well as the execution of profoundly significant military actions.

Working in advertising and public relations firms, Xers have a substantial influence on the promotional and advertising campaigns which bombard us daily. Xers are magazine editors and junior publishing executives, shaping the pages on news-stands and in book stores.

Xer teachers in our schools are educating the next generation. In public interest and non-profit foundations, public service organizations, government agencies, and the busy offices of some of the most powerful political leaders in the country, Xers have already started to shape policy and procedure.

THIS GENERATION ILLUMINATES THE POST-MODERN WORKPLACE

There is no denying that Generation X is playing an increasingly critical role in every sphere of the post-modern

7

workplace. Too many Xers are being poorly managed and the costs are too high to leave this problem unremedied. When managers fail to understand the needs and expectations of Xers and are therefore unable to manage Xers effectively, they diminish one of the most valuable resources at their disposal. These managers need to learn from the smart managers who take the time to understand Xers for who we really are, the managers who are bringing out the best in Generation X—and tapping into our unique creative power.

I will introduce you to Star Xers in an effort to clear away the many popular misperceptions about our generation.

First, you will see that Xers are not disloyal and uncommitted as so many people claim, but rather we are cautious investors in a world which has taught us to expect little from institutional relationships.

Second, I would like to correct the misperception that Xers have short attention spans and explain that Xers want so many answers to so many questions from so many sources in such a hurry because our learning and communication skills were shaped by the forces of the information revolution.

Third, you will see that the intense attitude expressed by so many Xers is not arrogance, but rather a powerful independence which grows out of a life experience in which we have always felt we had only ourselves on whom to depend at a very dangerous and unstable time in history.

Fourth, I'll address the fact that dues paying is an obsolete concept for Xers who face an employment market which offers no hope of long-term job security with any one employer. Xers' impatience for short-term rewards is a quest for a new kind of work related security based on self-building.

DON'T MISINTERPRET POPULAR IMPRESSIONS

Managers who misconstrue Xers' style and perceive in Xers disloyalty, lack of commitment, short attention spans, arrogance and greediness for rewards are the same managers who are bringing out the worst in Xers. In this book, you will learn directly from Xers about the unacceptable management relationships which kill our motivation and productivity, make us uncooperative, angry and resentful, sink morale in the workplace, and make us quit our jobs in search of new managers. You will learn how Xers respond when managers undervalue our work, refuse to guide and teach us, fail to offer challenges, opportunities and rewards. You will read the words of frustrated Xers being held back by ineffective managers who are throwing away our future as well as their own.

My interviewees loved telling stories about the managers they hate and have hated. Like other Xers I have known, my interviewees described, with bitter relish, their contempt for managers who are ungenerous, unfair, abusive, or intrusive, who won't answer Xers' questions or offer any guidance, who fail to reward Xers and give proper credit for the results they produce. Xers were eager to talk with me about bad managers for the same reasons they talk with each other at work. They spend inordinate amounts of time and creative energy exploring the dynamics of bad management relationships because they are not able to maximize their creative talents in their work.

One Coping Mechanism: Sitting Around And Talking

People talked. People would sit around and talk about what total jerks some of the managers were. People would say, "Wait till you hear what that asshole did today." It was like a running joke. With some managers we didn't even know, we would have preconceived notions about them, because we would hear stories.
Program Analyst

By working together through their shared experiences, Xers attempt to learn better how to cope with bad managers and also how to avoid them in the future.

A REALITY CHECK ON BAD MANAGEMENT

Perhaps most of all, by talking about bad managers, Xers seek from each other a reality check on their own impressions—and confirmation that they are not alone in their experiences. In this book, you will hear first-hand what Xers are whispering about at work.

I will also share with you the success stories which Xers shared with me—success stories which stand as models of effective management relationships with Xers. You will learn how smart managers who understand the real needs and expectations of Xers are bringing out the best in Generation X. Xers describe managers who are winning the generation's loyalty and commitment by placing a high value on Xers and our work.

These managers build teams which support Xers as individuals. They facilitate Xers' learning on the job and maximize our special relationship with information. They support Xers' independence by encouraging our natural entrepreneurism and creativity. And they provide cost effective reward systems which make Xers more productive while offering us opportunities for self-building—the only form of job security still available in our world.

Whether they are success stories or stories of failed management relationships, the stories in this book are not mine. They are the stories of the Star Xers whom I interviewed. They belong to those Star Xers and to my readers. Whether you are managing Generation X or Generation X being managed, you will find a story like yours in this book. Whether you recognize yourself in these pages or not, I hope you will gain valuable perspective by comparing yourself with those portrayed in management relationships both similar and dissimilar to your own. In these portrayals are vivid depictions of the rules and guidelines for managing Xers.

WHERE THIS BOOK FITS IN THE MANAGEMENT CANON

I think of this book as a necessary contribution to the steadily growing genre of books which offer advice on the subject of managing human resources. The human resource of Generation X presents managers with unique demands.

The management book genre is an outgrowth of a literature developed after World War II when it became increasingly clear to observers that the principal resource to be managed in the late twentieth-century workplace would be human beings. Some management theorists fit people into their charts and graphs, just as they do with inanimate resources like buildings, machinery, and raw materials—to these theorists, people are a terribly inefficient resource because our patterns of response are not automated.

By the 1950s, a more persuasive and more influential line of thought in management theory, built on the work of behavioral psychology, offered a more humanistic approach to management. Humanistic management theory was aimed at managing the Organization Man generation, the Depression-babies who were parents to the Baby Boomers and grandparents to Generation X. What was ground breaking about this work was that it treated management issues as a matter of human relations.

Not surprisingly, a new line of thought, known as motivational management theory, flourished in response to the malaise-ridden economy of the seventies, when managers struggled with unmotivated Baby Boomers entering a workplace which they found profoundly disappointing.

MOTIVATIONAL THEORY AND BEHAVIORAL PSYCHOLOGY: BOOMER STAPLES

The motivational theorists, also borrowing from humanistic psychology and behavioral science, argued that the keys to motivating employees were not to be found in money, hours and working conditions, but rather in treating employees with respect, allowing them to develop their own abilities and to work with and be valued by a cohesive team. Of course, these theories resonated strongly with the employee motivation problems which managers were dealing with in the seventies, when disgruntled Boomers dominated the work force.

The dominance of the Boomer ethos extended into the eighties and is reflected in perhaps the most famous management book of the decade, Tom Peters and Robert H. Waterman's *In Search of Excellence*. *In Search of Excellence* also showed the heavy influence of behavioral psychology, urging managers to "support champions" in the workplace as part of a strategy for developing a "corporate capacity for innovation."

Peters and Waterman based their conclusions about management on their study of forty-three "excellent" companies, defined by their consistent financial out-pacing of competitors over a twenty year period.

By 1987, two-thirds of Peters' and Waterman's "excellent" companies had stumbled into financial trouble, leaving only fourteen companies which still fit their initial definition of "excellence." The deterioration of twenty-nine "excellent" companies does not, by itself, undermine Peters' and Waterman's lessons for management. It does, however, call into question the methodology of studying management technique from the company perspective alone—from the standpoint of the manager and not the managed.

A GENERATION HAS APPEARED SINCE PETERS AND WATERMAN SEARCHED FOR EXCELLENCE

Of course, when *In Search of Excellence* was first published, the oldest members of Generation X had not even graduated from college. Indeed, no one has yet published a book addressing the particular demands of managing Generation X. Is it necessary to devote an entire book to the management needs of a new generation? In very general terms, much of the advice espoused by older management experts is applicable to managing Xers: demand personal responsibility, build goal-centered teams, develop the potential of each employee, support champions, reward innovation, and celebrate success.

My goal in writing this book is to spotlight the particular needs and expectations of the people my age who are playing increasingly critical roles in the workplace, particularly the implications of managing the Star Xers whom you will meet in this book. I was also committed to avoiding the tired approach of studying management technique from the standpoint of the manager. I wanted to study management at the source—to report directly how Xers are being managed and how it is affecting our work.

My instincts led me to an approach which most resembles journalistic sociology—I decided to base my book on the content of interviews with Xers themselves. The format of this book is designed to share with readers the actual words of the Xers whom I interviewed—to share wisdom from the most direct source possible about the ways in which various management techniques affect Xers' work as well as our attitudes about work.

The lessons for management which this book offers are somewhat consistent with the teachings of humanistic and motivational management theory to date. However, as you'll read in Chapter 1, Xers' expectations about work are different from those of prior generations and that means what we need from managers is also different.

As the Xers who speak in Chapter 3 of this book confirm, a great many managers are not rising to the particular challenge of managing Xers. Unable to bring out the best in the Xers who work for them, these managers are squandering one of their most valuable resources.

What this book offers that no management book has offered before is an up-close view of the management relationships which Xers are experiencing in the workplace every day. *Managing Generation X* offers an approach to managing Xers which is based on Xers' own first hand evaluations of managers, as well as Xers' first hand advice and recommendations to employers about how we should be managed.

Managing Generation X is a forum in which Star Xers speak for ourselves about our attitudes toward work and our experiences being managed. It is also an opportunity for readers to get to know Star Xers for who we really are and to learn directly from Xers about how different management techniques affect our work. This book provides managers with a guide to maximizing the value of the X variable in the equation of the bottom line.

FOUR CONSISTENT THEMES EMERGED

In almost all of the stories these Xers tell, the same issues keep arising over and over again:

- Belonging—is this a team where I can make a meaningful contribution?

- Learning—do I have sufficient access to information?

- Entrepreneurship—is there room in my work to define problems, develop solutions at my own pace, and produce my own results?

- Security—am I able to monitor the success rate of my performance, my status at work, and the return on my investment?

In the vast majority of the management relationships described to me by the Xers whom I interviewed, the answer to most of these questions was a resounding "No."

Some would be quick to point out that it is easier to criticize the status quo than it is to propose specific changes—the corollary is that there are powerful lessons to be learned in our errors. I hope to show that I am as committed to learning from success as from failure by focusing also on Xers' stories about effective managers who have inspired them to give their best.

SOME CONTEXT WILL GROUND THE COMING CHAPTERS

As you read this book, I hope you will keep in mind the historical position in which Xers find ourselves. Having grown up with a shrewd awareness of financial insecurity, Xers are uniquely cautious about investing our valuable abilities where they might not be appreciated.

Because Xers start out skeptical about the value of institutional relationships, managers who undervalue Xers reinforce that skepticism and encourage Xers to withhold our loyalty as well as our best work. Moreover, because Xers cannot count on job security as a reward for our hard work, we need to be entrepreneurial with our abilities—Xers need to find, in our work, opportunities to invest in ourselves, to build our personal assets.

That is why Xers find it so frustrating to work in environments where there is no room to learn and grow, which damage our self-esteem, where we are given no ownership of our work, not able to develop our creative abilities or produce our own results, and where there are scarce rewards for working hard.

At a time when the job market is so flush with eager young people looking for work, it easy for managers to think they don't have to worry about the needs of their employees—beggars can't be choosers. Don't give in to this kind of thinking. The fact is, in any job market, lazy management will result in low morale and high turnover, increased inefficiency and diminished quality. What is more, Xers, in particular, respond adversely to bad management.

If managers do not focus more directly on the particular management needs of Xers, companies will continue to pay the exacting price of losing the talents and innovations of a whole generation. But, for those who care enough to understand, a world of stunning possibilities is waiting to be seized.

CHAPTER 1:

Who Are These Xers In Your Office...And What Do We Want?

A GROUP SUBJECT TO MUCH SCRUTINY

Generation X, the group of Americans born between 1963 and 1981, has been subjected for the last few years to an increasingly voluminous popular discourse of disparagement. There is a widespread misconception among the public that Xers are mostly slackers, dropping out of the rat race to sponge off of our parents or barely surviving in low-pay, low-status, short-term "McJobs."

The truth is that there are millions of Star Xers doing critical work in important positions in every field imaginable. Yet, Star Xers are subject to many of the same popular misperceptions of our style as our peers who decide to sit out the rat race because the burdens outweigh the benefits. The greatest impact comes at the hands of managers who misunderstand the way Xers operate and are therefore unable to manage Xers effectively.

No one had heard of "Generation X" before the early 1990s. In the early 1980s, there had been a minor punk rock band that used the name. A few years later, Xer Douglas Coupland was doing a hip cartoon called *Generation X* for a Canadian newspaper. In 1991 Coupland published a novel with the same title about a group of jaded twentysomethings who had dropped out of the rat race because the Baby Boomers had devoured all the good stuff, leaving Xers with a future of "McJobs" and "Lessness." That same year, authors William Strauss and Neil Howe published a non-fiction book called *Generations* that contrasted predictable Baby Boom and less predictable post-Baby Boom demographics.

By that time, "Generation X" was common parlance among advertising executives, who used the term as a code-word for some fifty-million people who were considered difficult to pin down as a target market.

By 1993, it was official: the successors to the Baby Boom were being called "X" by *Time, Newsweek, BusinessWeek* and *Fortune.*

Why did the enigmatic "X" stick as a label for the generation? Some have called Xers a lost generation, claiming that we lack the same kind of historically distinguishable characteristics which mark preceding generations like the Baby Boomers and the Depression-babies. One observer even calls for a "new language" just to describe us. Still others insist that the growing effort to figure out Generation X is hopeless.

THE POPULAR MEDIA DIDN'T HESITATE TO STEREOTYPE X

Despite the alleged elusiveness of the X generation, the media has had no trouble settling on cliches to characterize Xers. Since the term "Generation X" first appeared, Xers have been described in the mainstream media as "cynical mopes," "sullen and contemptuous," "impetuous," "naive," "arrogant," "short on attention" and "materialistic," not to mention numerous virtually synonymous and equally unflattering variations.

One survey of the print media's coverage of Generation X, conducted by University of Rochester students under the direction of media consultant Nancy Woodhull, concluded that the vast majority of the portrayals of Generation X have been unduly negative. These depictions don't sit well with Xers, leading many observers to the further conclusion that Xers hate being labelled at all.

Whether any generation can really be captured by a single set of adjectives is, of course, highly questionable. However, more and more people are trying to figure out where Xers fit into their particular equation because Xers are coming of age as a generation and assuming an increasingly important role in society.

WHY EVERYONE WANTS TO LABEL X

The advertising industry spotted us first because money talks and fifty-million Xers are too big a market to ignore. In politics, Xers' increasing significance became clear during the 1992 presidential campaign when Bill Clinton (a Baby Boomer) donned his sunglasses and played the saxophone for us on the Arsenio Hall Show. *The Washington Post* identified the Xer vote as one of the four key factors responsible for the election of President Clinton.

How are managers fitting Xers into their equations in the workplace? Surveys of Baby Boomers who are managing Xers in a variety of white-collar fields, including one survey reported in *Fortune* magazine, reveal that Boomer managers find Xers to be disloyal, not sufficiently deferential to authority, short on attention, lacking commitment to work, arrogant, unwilling to go the extra mile, not willing to pay our dues, and overly concerned with finding fun and personal fulfillment in our work. These misconceptions undermine the ability of managers to maximize the potential value of Xers in the workplace.

WHAT THIS BOOK AIMS TO DO

The first task of this book, then, is to clear away the misperceptions and misinterpretations surrounding Generation X. The primary reason so many managers are failing to understand Xers is that managers' interpretations of Xers' behavior and attitudes is shaped, in one way or another, by Baby Boomers. First, Boomer managers are the authority figures in the workplace closest in age to Xers—that is why most companies put Boomer managers in charge of Xers and take most of their cues about managing Xers from these same Boomers. Second, Baby Boomers themselves mistakenly see reflections of their own youth in the Xers they are managing. Third, older managers remember that when Boomers hit the working world they too were a rather disgruntled lot of twentysomethings, and assume that the issues troubling us and the attitudes they perceive in us are much the same as with Boomers twenty years ago.

Both Boomer managers and older managers perceive in Xers the same tendencies that Baby Boomers exhibited when they were in their twenties. They think that Xers' discontent is merely a function of youthful naivete, that it's just a phase which will pass. Proponents of this view believe that, just like the Baby Boomers, Xers are bound to grow up at some point and realize that we cannot play the game by our own rules.

It is easy to see why this explanation makes sense to people familiar with the archetypal life experience of Baby Boomers. After all, Boomers are the generation which gave us hippies turned yuppies. Boomers played a starring role in the civil rights marches, anti-war protests, LSD parties and love-ins of the anti-materialist, anti-establishment sixties. The harsh reality of trying to make a living in the inflation-ridden economy of the seventies was sufficiently sobering for Boomers that, by the eighties, they were prepared to play a new starring role—this time as corporate tools in the greed decade. For Boomers, the anti-establishment spirit of the 1960s turned, over the course of time, into a conservative "realism."

Even Boomers who sat out the countercultural revolution look back on their own period of youthful rebellion with a mixture of idealistic nostalgia and gentle disapproval. Now that these Boomers are managers themselves, they and their older colleagues are waiting for Xers to come to our senses so that everybody can get back to work as usual.

DON'T JUDGE A GROUP BY ITS TWENTIES

The first crucial lesson of this book is that Xers may look like Boomers did in their twenties, but the vast differences in the historical experiences of Boomers and Xers give Xers a fundamentally different psychological profile which has dramatic implications for our needs and expectations of managers. The ongoing effort to define and understand Generation X is not solely the result of an advertising industry brainchild, but rather is motivated by subtle but real historical differences which make Xers quite different from Baby Boomers. Managers will not figure out how to fit Xers into their equations until they realize that Xers may have been born and bred in the Boomer lifestyle, but began our working lives during the post-eighties stage of American economic decline.

Xers are not like the flower children who took forever to grow up, but we have been influenced by them. The contrast between Boomers and Xers is instructive. The Baby Boom lasted from 1946 to the early 1960s, when Boomers themselves began to have children. Whereas Xers were born during a period of steady decline in American global power (kicked off by the Viet Nam War and punctuated by the Iranian hostage crisis), Baby Boomers were born in the era of American world preeminence which followed World War II.

THE WORLD AS BABY BOOMERS SAW IT

After World War II, with much of Europe and Asia in shambles, the United States enjoyed unprecedented levels of economic growth and increased prosperity: Per capita income grew in the fifties by 48 percent, home ownership increased by 50 percent, the labor force grew steadily, those fitting into the economic category of "middle class" reached 60 percent. Boomers were raised to expect a high and steadily increasing standard of living. Meanwhile, the workplace roles to which Boomers could look forward were becoming increasingly complex, demanding more and more education and training.

Luckily, their parents were doing well enough on the whole that they could afford to provide the Baby Boomers with more years of education per person than any other generation in history, also providing the student populations behind much of the late-sixties radicalism. As the parents of middle-class Boomers invested greater time and money in their children's education (and future standard of living), the childhood of these Baby Boomers was often extended well into their twenties—a longer maturation period than any other generation in history and another sharp contrast to the truncated childhood of Xers, exposed at the youngest ages to the every day realities of adult life.

By the time Baby Boomers were leaving university campuses to enter the working world at an unprecedented late age, the economy was not as friendly as it had looked in their youth. The annual increase in the labor force doubled with the entry of Boomers, creating great competition for jobs. Between 1964 and 1974, when the first wave of Boomers hit the labor force, the average annual increase was 1.74 million, compared with an average of .88 million between 1953 and 1964. International economic competition was heating up as Japan and Europe began to produce vigorously again, catching the fat-cats of American industry off guard. The American economy of the seventies was subject to the great inflationary pressures of oil embargoes and war-time and post-war military budgets—the first impression of economics for Generation Xers, but a dramatic let-down for Baby Boomers. Rather than exceeding their parents' standard of living as they clearly expected to do, Boomers graduating in the seventies were the first college graduates ever to see their relative earnings decline in relation to that of their parents.

Economic disappointment was only one field of smashed expectations for the Baby Boomers. The ideals of Boomer childhood, conditioned by family life, cold-war nationalism, and idealistic patriotism had been transformed by drastic cultural changes—the wave of assassinations destroying faith in the moral order, Viet Nam and Watergate disrupting the political order, and civil rights, the youth movement and feminism redefining even the most intimate aspects of the social order.

BOOMERS TURN THEIR FOCUS INWARD

It is no wonder Boomers made the seventies into the "Me" decade. Boomers had rejected the 1950s' bias toward institutions and institutional values in favor of experimentation with radical, universal social change. When the communalism of the sixties proved to be a disappointment and the

Boomer generation began to take over the previously scorned reins of status quo power, they began to focus on creating a highly personal, though still theoretical, sense of well-being as a way of adjusting to the responsibilities of adulthood.

Then came Ronald Reagan, who embodied the fading American dream and promised to make it true again. Reagan offered Baby Boomers a chance to realize their childhood expectations after all—after a long dark night it was finally Morning in America. Perhaps the genius of Reagan was his ability to end the Baby Boomers' generational tantrum by making the eighties into the big party they had been expecting since the fifties. Boomers' history puts into perspective the fact that so many of them so easily accepted and participated in the greed ethos of the eighties. First, career was never the center stage of Boomers' rebellion anyway. Second, by the eighties, many Boomers saw the critical issues of their youth (civil rights, Viet Nam, feminism, sexual freedom) as moot. Third, after struggling to make a living during the seventies, most Boomers were ready to embrace institutions again (especially ones which might help them pay the bills).

THE WORLD AS XERS SEE IT

Xers' experience of this shift from the ethos of the 1970s to that of the 1980s, fundamentally different from the experience of Baby Boomers, is crucial to understanding the unique perspective of Generation X. Xers have inherited the Boomer's late twentieth-century disillusionment, without having had the opportunity for youthful idealism.

Very few Xers were old enough to participate in the spendthrift eighties, but we were interested spectators. The seventies didn't give us a lot of heroes—older Xers could tell that we were growing up in a second-rate imitation of the 1960s and younger Xers saw the 1960s as little more than ancient history. As the icon for the 1980s, Ronald Reagan provided a brief, ersatz version of idealism for this generation.

The oldest Xers, who were old enough to vote in 1984, turned out in lower numbers than any new voting group in history. However, those who did vote supported Reagan by a substantial margin. The upbeat mood of Morning in America was more appealing than the cultural malaise of the seventies, consciousness-raising included. But Xers proved to be the volatile voting block Republican pollsters worried we would be, splitting evenly in 1988 and then, after it became undeniable that the eighties had been a hoax, voting heavily for Clinton in 1992. The primary issue influencing the political climate in 1992 was that of jobs and personal financial struggle, or in the parlance of the day: "It's the economy, stupid." In 1994 many Xers stayed home again to rethink our political loyalties. Where we will be by 1996 is anybody's guess—and the worry of every politician.

XERS TURN THEIR FOCUS TO PARADOXES

The volatility of Xers' political loyalties is an example of our uncertainty about the value of institutional relationships. Growing up in a habitat of rapid change and social atomization, without the backdrop of 1950s and 1960s idealism, Xers have had sparse opportunities to witness or experience enduring affiliations of any kind—social, geographical, religious or political. Our own family structures, and those of our peers, have not been reliable. We are unlikely to have spent our childhoods in one community—and even if we did, our childhoods were marked by the characteristics of suburban diaspora and the evisceration of community centers. For these reasons, even our friendship circles have always been in flux, shifting along with forces beyond our control.

As routinely as we acclimated to new friends and new homes and new schools, we witnessed vivid images of social, economic and political change while surfing on an ever increasing number of television channels. Our social attitudes were learned amidst the competing discourses of family values and gay pride, prime-time sex and AIDS awareness, the War on Drugs and the cocaine deaths of sports heroes. Meanwhile, how could we help feeling vulnerable? Xers were well versed in the threat of nuclear war, the reality of environmental decay, and all the acute dangers to children posed in a perverse world—the abductions of the Milk Carton Kids, child abuse, and the rest.

Xers learned to worry about our economic future by watching politicians play fast and loose with the national debt—the economic problems of the seventies seeming to disappear overnight with voodoo economics, the spendthrift profligacy of the eighties evaporating into fiscal scarcity after America surpassed its credit limit.

POLITICS AND CULTURE AS MANAGEMENT GUIDES

Xers reached political awareness in an atmosphere where heroes, and even empires, in real life were being made and unmade faster than they were in our favorite one-hour television dramas. Notwithstanding the cultural force of Ronald Reagan, most Xers never saw politics as being worth our time and energy—much less as center-stage for expressing our selfhood.

If U.S. presidents define their times, few Xers can even recall a time when politics was not contextualized by corruption (Nixon), humiliation (Carter), surrealism (Reagan), ineffectiveness (Bush) or disappointment (Clinton). That is one reason why eligible Xers vote in lower percentages than any other generation in history and are portrayed by many as politically apathetic.

While certain political issues (the national debt, pollution, and AIDS) are definitely important to Xers, Xers see our careers as the key struggle we face in our twenties and early thirties. In contrast to the Baby Boomers, Xers see working for a living, as opposed to working for social justice, as most fundamental to our self-definition.

We have little reason to be idealistic—nothing in Xers' life experience has remained the same long enough to inspire our unquestioning belief. What we believe in most is change and uncertainty. The vulnerability inherent in our changing environment has conditioned us to attend first to our own well-being, leaving little time for intangibles like ideology. Rather than looking to distant political leaders (whom we barely trust) to make us safe, Xers are looking to ourselves, as we always have.

WE HAVE LITTLE RELIANCE ON EXTERNAL FORCES

In a world in which everything external is shifting so fast, it has been difficult for Xers to rely at all on external forces, much less find self-definition there. So, Xers have learned to define ourselves in terms of our own creative abilities. Since childhood we have found our existential proof by defining and solving for ourselves the problems of everyday life, from making frozen dinners in the microwave when our parents had to work late to making friends in a new school when our parents moved to figuring out the challenges of a new video game to keep us company when we were alone.

As our everyday problems became more complex, we learned new problem-solving skills, our repertoires developing in sync with the information revolution. To this day, our own resourcefulness, and our comfort with new technologies, remain our most reliable allies for coping in an uncertain world.

CREATIVITY EQUALS SAFETY TO X

For Xers, opportunities for creative expression provide us with the psychologically important, and very practical, reassurance that we will be able to survive tomorrow. Working for a living, therefore, is for Xers the most natural venue for staking out a position of safety in a dangerous world.

Xers' proclivity to look for safety in work is about more than self-definition. It is also very pragmatic. We started thinking about working for a living as the lame images of the seventies turned into the eighties' media representations of prodigious financial success and materialism.

When that other icon of the 1980s, Michael J. Fox, came along, Xers thought his portrayal of cold materialism, business-like conservatism, and dry humor were new and cool but not ironic. Just as Reagan's upbeat mood was more appealing to Xers than Carter's malaise, so the success orientation of yuppie culture, metaphorized by the Fox character Alex Keaton, was more appealing than the struggling eccentrics of the seventies—like the characters played by John Travolta in *Welcome Back Kotter* or Jimmie Walker in *Good Times*.

The yuppie culture of the eighties permeated Xers' youth, but we only saw the pay-off from a distance. We watched it mostly on television, always—always hearing that faint, nagging echo about how politicians were leaving us with this unimaginably huge debt. When the reality of that debt caught up with the economy in the late eighties, Xers were starting to enter the job market. The sense of irony which has come to be associated with Generation X stems from the incongruities of these parallel economic and cultural transformations.

Understanding the shift from the lame seventies to the hollow promise of the eighties to the harsh realities of the nineties is crucial for those who wish to understand Generation X.

XERS ALREADY HAVE AN EFFECT ON THE BOTTOM LINE

Because of our social, economic and cultural history, Xers have been acutely focused on career issues from the time we were young children. Our concerns about the seemingly erratic prospects of making a living in an unstable economy have been confirmed by our historical experience—culminating for now in a period of financial scarcity when making a living is not a sure thing for anyone. It is certainly true that many Xers find themselves stuck in McJobs—this is a painful reality in a society with a declining standard of living. It is also true that Xers are dropping out of the rat race in large numbers—many have decided that, especially in a buyers' market, the rewards of certain jobs are just not worth the demands. Some drop-out Xers might live with their parents or with friends while they regroup. Still other Xers who have dropped-out and regrouped successfully are participating in the new entrepreneurial boom of the nineties by starting their own companies.

This book is not about the Xers who are dropping out. Rather, it is about the Xers who are staying in the rat race—and not in McJobs but in high powered positions in law, medicine, banking, scientific research, insurance, education, sales, accounting, the non-profit sector, politics, government service, the military, research, high-tech service industries, and manufacturing. Some are being managed well, but most are being managed poorly. The words of the Xers who speak in this book convinced me that the reason why most Xers are being managed poorly is because their managers fail to take Xers seriously. Managers who fail to take Xers seriously, who write-off Xers' discontent in the workplace, do so because they are operating under a fundamental misconception about us: they think that our style is a function of youthful naivete, rather than a function of precocious shrewdness.

The Money Centers Already Rely On Xers

> *Here is a financial giant relying more than you can imagine on a small army of super ambitious twentysomethings. These people are doing the critical work on some of the biggest deals in the international business world.*
>
> **Associate at a major investment bank**

THE VALUE OF GENERATION X IN THE MANAGEMENT EQUATION

If managers are going to take Xers seriously, they are going to have to get to know us for who we really are—grown-up, shrewd, and very valuable when managed well. The first step is to readjust some faulty interpretations.

First, Xers are not disloyal as we may appear to some managers. In fact, Xers are eager to make lasting contributions to institutions which welcome and value our investment. But, managers have to realize that Xers have grown up with the assumption that most institutional relationships are short-lived. Indeed, job security, per se—the idea of a lifelong relationship with an employer—is a feature of work that Xers only know of by reputation, as we will surely never experience it.

The disappearance of long-term institutional relationships is only one aspect of an entire habitat of rapid change in which Xers have formed our most basic coping mechanisms for life. Underlying Xers' seeming restlessness or disloyalty is a unique ability to adapt to change, which should be marshalled by managers as a powerful resource. If you read closely what Xers have to say in this book, you will see that Xers are actually great team players if we are accepted on our own terms.

Second, Xers do not have short attention spans, as so many managers seem to think. Rather, Xers are voracious learners who love to sort through and digest massive quantities of information at a very fast pace. Managers who want to understand Xers have to realize that Xers' style of interacting with information is a function of our immersion in the information revolution.

Remember, Xers have a different relationship to the mechanisms of the information revolution than older generations. We didn't have to get used to integrating information technology into our work habits. Information technology shapes the way we learn. What looks to many managers like a short attention span is, in fact, a rapid-fire style of information consumption, which makes Xers uniquely suited to the workplace of the future. If you read closely what Xers have to say in Chapter Six, you will see that, far from being short on attention, Xers are happiest when our work is a constant learning process.

Third, Xers are not arrogant or insolent. When managed properly, Xers are willing to go the extra mile, and then some. The fact is that Xers are fiercely independent and amazingly entrepreneurial. To understand Xers' fierce independence managers have to understand that Xers grew up with a powerful sense of personal danger. From the arms race, violent crime, drugs, and AIDS to the national debt, we have been exposed to a sense of constant jeopardy, as well as many patently false reassurances from figures of authority.

XERS DON'T SEEK ISOLATION...WE COME FROM IT

Managers need to remember that Xers are latchkey kids—we are used to taking care of ourselves and we are used to finding original solutions to intractable problems. What looks to managers like arrogance is, in fact, a natural entrepreneurism with our creative prowess which was self-nurtured during a childhood marked by less than optimal parental supervision. You will see that when managers allow Xers more autonomy in our work, Xers are profoundly determined to innovate.

Fourth, it makes no sense to say that Xers are not willing to pay our dues, although it is true that Xers are impatient for rewards and other indications that our hard work is being appreciated. The concept of paying one's dues depends on some notion of investment, on the idea that there is a long-term benefit somewhere in the bargain. Yet, Xers have little reason to believe in any long-term bargains.

Again, economic, environmental and social decay on a global level have always confronted Xers with the fungibility of Planet Earth, while the consumer culture of immediacy continually surrounds us with the markings of our own disposable life experience. When it comes to work, why should Xers believe in dues paying? No one is promising us job security, which is the implicit reward for paying dues. Expecting that Xers will pay dues in the traditional sense is unrealistic because employers have withdrawn their consideration for the bargain. Thus, managers need to shape a new bargain, offering a new system of rewards and a new kind of security in return for Xers' contributions.

Managers need to realize that Xers' impatience for rewards and recognition is really a function of the career insecurity imposed on us by the same economic forces which constrain employers. As it is with other institutions in our experience, Xers have no confidence that our employers offer enduring relationships. Xers are not willing to make investments with employers offering returns only in the long-term because there is no long-term. Blue-chip employment relationships are not available to Xers. This should explain for managers why Xers are always looking for short-term dividends on our work. Providing short-term dividends is the key to building a new system of rewards that instills confidence in Xers that our contributions are valued enough by managers to warrant our best efforts. However, those dividends are not necessarily financial.

Cash Is Great...But It Doesn't Mean Security

Money might keep me here for a while but that isn't going to make me feel like part of the team, it isn't going to get the very best work out of me. I guess what I really want is to be important to the team, to feel like my work is contributing to something of lasting value.
Associate at an investment bank

A NEW GENERATION LOOKS FOR A NEW EMPLOYMENT BARGAIN

Managers have to find a substitute for the long-term job security they have withdrawn if they hope to establish a new bargain with Xers. However, Xers are looking for a substitute far more complex than money. While this complicates the bargain, it also presents a wonderful opportunity for Xers and those managers who are willing to take part.

Because work is so critical to our self-definition, Xers seek management relationships which help us to invest in ourselves as lifelong proprietors of our creative abilities. This process, which I call self-building, is central to Xers' pursuit of a new self-based career security. Providing Xers with short-term dividends by making contributions to our self-building process demands the personal engagement of managers. Managers can contribute to Xers' self-building by providing the kind of feedback that facilitates learning, feedback which helps us to improve our future performance.

Managers can contribute by offering unfettered access to information, furnishing opportunities to work in new skill areas, and by teaching—all contributions which help Xers build our repertoires of valuable skills. Managers also contribute when they provide Xers with opportunities to define and solve problems, to demonstrate our resourcefulness, and prove ourselves with innovative results. These, and other ways of helping Xers to pursue a new self-based career security, are the most valuable short-term dividends managers can provide—dividends sure to attract the personal investment of Xers.

If you read closely what Xers have to say throughout this book, you will see that, given regular indications that our investment is paying-off, our ambition will drive us to go more than the extra mile.

CHAPTER 2:

Common Misconceptions About Generation X

XERS ARE NOT DISLOYAL

Does Xers' fierce independence make us the disloyal non-team players so many managers seem to think we are? Is it true that Xers have no lasting allegiances? These questions are off the mark because the concept of loyalty, allegiance, and belonging to a team has a different meaning to Xers than it does to those of prior generations. Both Xers' understanding of how we relate to our world and the way we experience belonging with respect to any kind of institution have been shaped by a habitat of rapid change, in which we have always been expected to adapt quickly to the demands of new situations. Perhaps the greatest continuity Xers know is discontinuity.

Xers matured to the mixed messages of post-industrial politics. We learned contempt for institutions in the echoes of Watergate, Three Mile Island, the Iranian hostage crisis, and

Iran-Contra. But, we desperately wanted to believe in the mythology of Reagan's Morning in America. Xers watched our fiscal future deteriorate through Carter's malaise and Reagan's spendthrift eighties only to land in the deep scarcity of the nineties.

When Xers tuned into world politics, Ronald Reagan was impugning the "evil empire" and, when we turned around, the Soviet empire was disintegrating. The maps we studied in high school and college are already obsolete. In the shadow of the unwinnable Viet Nam War, Xers watched with incredulity as CNN's version of the Gulf War looked like a video game mini-series.

WHAT IS BELONGING IN THE AGE OF MIRACLE AND WONDER?

Our cultural awareness got a false start during the imitation decade (the overly self-conscious and rather embarrassing seventies) and a false promise during the greed decade (the shameful eighties), so that Xers find ourselves, as adults in the nineties, with the responsibility to lead new trends having very little in our past from which to borrow. We grew up watching re-runs of *Star Trek* and the *Odd Couple*. We found images of ourselves in *The Brady Bunch*, then *Mork & Mindy* and then *Beverly Hills 90210*. We found ordinary heroes in *Hill Street Blues*, then *L.A. Law* and then *Law and Order*, science fiction heroes in *Star Trek: The Next Generation, Deep Space Nine*, and of course the *X-Files*. Our comic foils in *Saturday Night Live*, *In Living Color* and, most of all, *David Letterman*.

The music scene shifted to video, and split into a million pieces that defy easy analysis. Beatles songs became oldies and the Rolling Stones flirted with Disco. Julian Lennon performed in his own right. Paul Simon sang in harmony with African tribal musicians. Hardcore Rap became mainstream.

Kurt Cobain killed himself—and his widow became a star. Now we listen to groups as diverse as Pearl Jam and Snoop Doggy Dogg, Stone Temple Pilots and the Cranberries.

As the pace of our culture has been set by new technologies, so the pace of technological change in Xers' lifetime has been shocking. The mimeograph machines Xers remember from elementary school turned into high speed copiers by the time we got to high school. Two-pound adding machines were replaced by calculators the size of credit cards, credit cards became available like cotton candy, and TVs went from three channels to seventy-five.

THERE'S MORE THAN MONEY AT THE BOTTOM LINE

Growing up in a fast-paced and changing society, Xers have had fewer opportunities for developing long-term connections with lasting institutions. People no longer stay with the same church for very long, the same doctor, the same political party, or the same job. Divorce, multi-sexuality, and commuter marriages have reshaped our expectations of family and community life.

In terms of social values, what older generations found shocking or interesting, Xers take for granted—great diversity in family situations, lifestyle options, sexual preference, race, gender, political and religious orientation.

We grew up with divorced parents and single parents, with both parents working to maintain a threatened standard of living. Our friends and loved ones are becoming vegetarian, coming out of the closet, joining therapeutic movements, new age churches and Eastern religions, losing their jobs, losing their health insurance, terrified of AIDS—or flirting with it or dying of it—getting new jobs, shopping for better health care, and electing a President whose inauguration included an MTV Inaugural Ball.

XERS AREN'T AFRAID OF CHANGE—IT'S WHAT WE KNOW BEST

Because Xers have developed our survival instincts in a habitat of rapid change and unreliable institutional connections, Xers have a different way of belonging and developing allegiance than those of prior generations. Xers are also more cautious in choosing our connections, and examine institutions for very specific virtues before deciding to make a personal investment.

Because most Xers were not raised with institutional loyalties, we do not have a conditioned ethic of loyalty to institutions, nor do we have any expectation that institutions have reciprocal loyalties to offer. That is most true with institutional employers, who no longer offer job security. Thus, long-term loyalties based on such expectations do not come naturally to Xers.

Rather, Xers are capable of a learned loyalty to institutions and individuals which grows out of a more localized and immediate dynamic. Xers develop loyalty to institutions which reflect back to Xers our own value—institutions in which we can prove to others and confirm for ourselves that we have valuable contributions to make.

In a work environment, more than any other, where Xers will seek security and self-definition through opportunities to be creative, we experience belonging only to the extent that our specific contributions are noted and valued. Most Xers don't need to be the most or the only important person in an organization, but we do need to feel that our presence means something—Xers want to make an impact.

Far from being estranged from people and institutions, per se, Xers are able to mix, mingle, circulate and socialize. What is more, Xers are adaptable like chameleons—capable of making fast connections with diverse sorts of new people and new groups. The question for Xers is not whether we have the ability to connect with people and organizations, but whether we choose to connect with particular individuals and organizations.

One of the skills that makes Xers so adaptable is our ability to distinguish between affiliations which are likely to reflect back our own value and those which are not. At work, it is particularly easy to distinguish. Xers express our value by trying to make specific tangible contributions—we see our value proven in our ability to create valuable end-products or results.

When managers invite Xers to organize our work around specific contributions (valuable end-products), they are reflecting back Xers' expressions of value. Xers are eager to carve our initials in the tree: "X was here!" is not enough...

"X was here because X made a valuable contribution!"

One Straight Shooter Takes Aim

There Is great satisfaction when you can have an impact on something that is going to last and become independent and work on its own for the long term.
Strategic planner for a major clothing company

Success Means Everyone Feels Crucial In Some Way

When a team is successful at an important task and everybody gets to feel like they played a key role, everyone feels crucial in some way, that is the key to building a really strong team of these young officers.
Officer in the U.S. Armed Forces

XERS ARE NOT CYNICS

Managers have to stop mistaking Xers' cautious approach to institutions and seeming transience as an inability to form lasting allegiances. Rather, Xers use our adaptability to facilitate our scrutiny of various institutions, in search of institutions where we can belong. That is, institutions where we can make an impact. The fact is, the workplace is probably the most coherent social group available to most Xers. Xers are eager to find work environments which welcome and value our contributions enough to warrant our investment. As the words of the Xers who speak in this section make clear, if taken seriously and allowed to make our mark, Xers have a deeper loyalty to give than many. It is not the feigned loyalty habitual to a moot bargain, but rather a reasoned loyalty based on the very real prospect of seeing our value proven through valuable contributions.

"Part Of The Reason We Have Grown..."

Being part of something that is growing and watching it really go places makes me very happy. When I started here five and a half years ago it was nothing like it is today. I feel like my work is a big part of the reason why we have grown and been successful.
Vice president at a major investment bank

When managers organize Xers' work around responsibility for specific end-results, it is easier for Xers to be confident that the impact of our work is appreciated. Xers begin to identify with the success of our employers when we can see our accomplishments are valued and important parts of our employers' success. That identification is not based on a necessarily enduring relationship with the particular employer, but on the potentially enduring value of the contribution. Xers are like the Johnny Appleseeds of the workplace. Our end-results are like seedlings in our employers' landscapes. Managers who show they are likely to tend Xers' seedlings and feature them in the landscape are the managers who win Xers' finest contributions.

One Team Really Makes A Mark

It was a short-term association for me but it was like us against the world and our team was really going to make a mark. There was a lot of cooperation so that, within the team, everybody's own expertise fit in its own way. They gave me a lot of responsibility within the team, which I found exciting and rewarding because it allowed me to make a substantial contribution during the time I was there.

Research scientist in an electronics company

SHORT-TERM HEROISM: XERS WANT TO LEAVE CALLING CARDS IN THE FORM OF VALUABLE RESULTS

Even given short associations, Xers will use short periods of time to invest in the landscape, if we have a chance. Short-term associations can be wasted time for Xers. But, they seem like great opportunities when we can quickly leave a mark. Managers should seize Xers who are merely passing through as occasions to turn around short-term projects with very tangible end-products. Xers will adopt those projects like lost puppies and train them to jump through flaming hoops.

An X Ideal: Working Interactively, Brainstorming Ideas

We work interactively, brainstorming ideas, doing research, and thinking creatively and strategically about new business opportunities for the company. We then pull this together into presentations to the head of our group. I have actually presented to the president of the company in cases where I knew the most about a project or idea. I'll tell you, that is a huge incentive to do great work.

Business development associate in a major entertainment company

XERS LOOK FOR TEAMS BUILT AROUND INFORMATION

Xers thrive in teams that support the individual. Collaborative efforts are best organized around open information environments, where ideas can be exchanged openly and goals set as a group. Everyone talks about brainstorming. When brainstorming results in an end-product, even if that end-product is just a presentation, Xers value the collaborative experience. Xers don't need to be the leaders in a group in order to play a driving role. We do need to feel included in the process of shaping team goals and we do need to have a concrete role in implementing team goals. Without those features, it doesn't look like a team to Xers. Xers don't want to sit on the bench.

Liking The Role Of Command Central

Even when he is traveling, my manager calls in: he starts the conversation with "I'm in my car" and he ends with "You're in charge." We are like command central. That makes me feel really critical to the company and it makes every one of my projects seem important. They are just really good at making people feel like they are important to the company and that our work is important.

Analyst at a small investment bank

Working Collaboratively Makes Risk-taking Easier

Everybody has a lot of respect for the other members of the team. We work collaboratively. We always work from the goal. I feel comfortable that I can say anything I want to in this process. I feel like it is worthwhile to speak up and contribute, it is safe to take a risk. I am definitely able to have a strong influence on the work we do and it feels good to see my more innovative ideas implemented.

Education policy aide in the office of one of our nation's Governors

XERS KNOW RISK-TAKING IS THE KEY TO INNOVATION

Collaborative teams, which encourage participation and provide opportunities for individual accomplishment, can be great sources of innovation. Such teams offer Xers spheres in which our innovations can be tested safely. Safety promotes risk-taking. Risk-taking promotes innovation. Imagine the innovations lost to industry every day because they're stifled in group discussions for fear of disturbing the status quo. It is a terrible thought.

What Is Knowledge In A Perennial Information Revolution?

I want to be working in an environment where I face a new challenge every day, where I am learning constantly, where I have the opportunity to wrestle with the hottest new developments and expand my repertoire of skills so that I am always keeping up with technology.

Electrical engineer

XERS DO NOT HAVE SHORT ATTENTION SPANS

One critical ground of misunderstanding between managers and Xers seems to be about the way in which Xers interact with information. To many managers, it seems that Xers have painfully short attention spans, that we ask too many questions, that we always want to know more than we need to know, that we want to be spoon-fed information. This interpretation could not be more mistaken.

The truth is that Xers are veritable learning machines. We devour information, soaking it up, sorting it, warehousing some, discarding some, leaving some on the back burner to simmer and some more on the front burner to boil. Don't look now, Xers are reaching into the cupboard to open a whole new can of worms.

Xers have developed a rapid-fire style of interacting with information because the information revolution has shaped the way we think. Don't forget, we didn't have time to develop pre-information revolution learning habits because the information revolution was approaching full speed by the time we learned to read. Boomers and older generations enter the information highway gradually (if at all), as if merging with traffic.

Xers were born in the infobahn's fast lane.

This generation is used to nearly infinite information coming at us in rapid-fire doses. Think of music videos, *Miami Vice*, CNN, ESPN, C-SPAN, Court TV, the Weather Channel, and VCRs. Vivid images of constant change: Revolution, war, terrorism, diplomacy, politics from Carter to Reagan to Clinton, famine, fire, earthquakes, floods, violent crime, sicko-crime, kangaroo courts, urban riots, oil spills, nuclear accidents, New Coke, Coke Classic, Caffeine Free Diet Pepsi, Jolt, Gary Hart, Michael Jackson, Tonya Harding, the making and unmaking of heroes, the making and remaking of meaning.

Xers are the children of video games and computers. Xers learned to write using word processors with which words, sentences and paragraphs can be rearranged, deleted, and replaced, changes can be made and errors erased—all without effort. Xers barely know what card-catalogues look like because on-line indexes can search the shelves of a dozen libraries within moments. Xers developed our research skills using computers capable of doing in a matter of hours what used to take weeks or months.

AN ASSET OF X: A FUNDAMENTALLY DIFFERENT PERSPECTIVE

, When Xers apply for jobs, we use database and mail-merge programs to send out resumes and cover letters to employers. To communicate, Xers are comfortable using E-Mail, fax machines, voice mail, beepers and cellular phones. As teenagers, Xers created a market for call-waiting and more. Xers' life experience makes us uniquely suited to the information age in which the ability to adjust with technological change is increasingly important. That makes Xers uniquely suited to and inestimably valuable to the workplace of the future.

Those managers who think that Xers have short attention spans understand neither our relationship to information nor the way we learn. Xers have learned to cope with information quickly and efficiently because of the sheer volume of information fired at us since we began learning how to think. The information revolution is just beginning and, if managers don't want to lose pace, they had better figure out where Xers fit in their equation.

XERS PLACE A PREMIUM ON FLEXIBILITY

Xers are in a hurry to learn for good reason—in an era where technological change is a constant, there is a premium on quick mastery. What is more, the ability to cope with massive quantities of information quickly is sure to be the key survival skill of the twenty-first century workplace. Xers cannot afford to stop learning. That is why Xers demand so much information and increasingly look to managers to play the role of teachers.

As the Xers who speak in the following section make clear, far from having short attention spans, we need managers who can keep pace with our voracious appetites for information by constantly refueling the work environment with endless supplies of challenging experience, new projects, new skill areas, new technology, new interpretations, and new meaning. Finally, it is easy to see that managers who engage Xers in learning relationships win our deepest loyalties. The reason is that managers willing to teach Xers are investing in our self-building—they are helping Xers to become more valuable proprietors of our creative abilities.

As a result, teaching managers enjoy mutually beneficial relationships with Xers who are highly motivated, Xers whose skills are improving routinely, and Xers who are less likely to move along in search of new managers. Xers are likely to stay around as long as we are still learning at a steady pace.

Doing Anything In Order To Learn

I am willing to work on anything in order to learn. I need to be regularly working in new areas. I want to be working in an environment where I can constantly learn from the knowledge and experience of others and expand my abilities.

Human resources department for a chemical manufacturer

Make Sure We Get Valuable Experience

If a manager cares about my career, about me as a person, goes out of his or her way to keep me informed, to give me access to maximum information, to make sure that I get valuable experience, that is a manager that is going to get my best work and my total loyalty. With managers like that I have always taken a lot more initiative, more responsibility, and gotten more involved in my work and it definitely affects how willing I am to work hard for someone.

Analyst at a major credit card company

FOR XERS, INFORMATION YIELDS INITIATIVE AND RESPONSIBILITY

Xers want to learn by doing. That doesn't mean throwing Xers into sink or swim situations. That means providing Xers with clear end-goals and every possible information resource necessary to work toward those goals. Information resources include libraries, selected materials and on-line sources. But that is not enough. Challenging Xers with assignments in new skill areas takes more up-front management time. But, it is worth the up-front management time to help Xers learn and grow at work. Armed with new skills and motivated by the learning process, Xers will gladly assume new responsibilities and meet challenges with greater initiative. As long as we are learning, we will keep adding value—gladly—in the form of tangible end-results.

Looking For More Training

When my manager wants me working in areas where I already have experience, that keeps me from growing and learning. I am always looking for more training in new areas. I want to be learning new skills and new information whenever possible.

Marketing manager for a major financial services firm

"Put Me On Projects Which Allow Me To Learn"

A manager has to assign work that I may not have the skills for yet, so I can learn new skills. Rather than placing me only where my skills were, put me in projects which would allow me to learn, to make mistakes, and to learn from other engineers. I want a manager who seems genuinely concerned with my need to learn, with my need to be exposed to as much information as possible, and who can get me the kind of work and experience that I wanted to gain, who recognizes that career development is important.

Electrical engineer

Experimentation Cures Inexperience

One very good thing is when managers try to emphasize that you can experiment and go into a field where you are inexperienced. That promotes risk-taking. The idea is not to narrow people, (it's) to keep people interested because they are able to do something new. I can only feel satisfied if I can keep learning about new aspects of the business on a consistent basis.

Executive in a development program at a large chemical company

Each New Operation—Each New Patient—Is A Challenge

I love being pushed and I love pushing myself. Each new operation, each new patient, is a constant challenge. Even if it is a simple case or something I have done before, I can do it more smoothly, with more economy of motion. There is always more to learn. I want to learn the style and art of medicine and surgery—not just the technique. As I go on in residency, I am doing more and more sophisticated operations. It is a lot of pressure, but necessary pressure. I love it.

Physician in surgical residency

The Sponge Approach To Absorbing Information

I was told to become a sponge and absorb as much information and methodology as I could. I was promised that someone would be training me in every aspect of the job. I need to go after and absorb as much information as I can. I want to learn.
Management consulting staff at a big six accounting firm

The Best Managers Are Good Teachers

The worst managers resort to "Gee, it would be faster if I do this myself," under the time crunch and just give the analysts more menial work. Or (they say,) "Go figure it out." Maybe (they do this) because they don't know themselves. I know that the best managers I had were the ones who were good teachers.
Associate at an investment bank

XERS ARE NOT ARROGANT

Another reason why so many managers have a hard time fitting Xers into their management equation in the workplace is that they misinterpret Xers' fierce individualism and entre-preneurial style as arrogance. Again, in marked contrast to the Baby Boomers, Xers' individualism has very little to do with rebelling against authority—our self-assuredness comes from a powerful sense that we have been able largely to fend for ourselves.

We are also acutely tuned in to our need to, in fact, fend for ourselves. We learned how to be "selves" in a society which increasingly atomizes the individual, all the while confronting him or her with a growing sense of personal danger. Xers' ability to navigate our "selves" in a seemingly dangerous world is key to our self-definition. Because work is such an important sphere of self-definition for Xers, a degree of freedom to navigate our "selves" in our work is the optimal condition for Xers.

Most Xers are the children of Boomers, parents who were so deeply involved with their own "selves," working by day and raising consciousness by candlelight, that they were unable to give us their full attention—leaving us alone much of the time. And, like their own parents, our parents listened to Dr. Spock—they were permissive, they gave us room to explore. While both parents got ready for work every morning, Xers made cereal for breakfast and stared at photos of our peers on milk cartons, our own MIAs.

A YOUTH FORMED BY SELF-SUFFICIENCY

Xers went to school to be tracked—to excel or be left in the dust. After school, Xers took care of other Xers, watched TV, played computer games, had boyfriends, had girlfriends, ate junk food, smoked pot, got pregnant, got abortions, got our own birth-control, made frozen dinners in the microwave, watched some more TV, did some homework, a little more TV.

Whatever we did, Xers spent a lot of time alone. That is one reason why Xers actually believe in the self. Personal responsibility is more than a slogan to Xers because the concept resonates powerfully with our childhood experience of solitude.

Of course, the fad-quotient of the "self" is not lost on Xers: self-help, self-improvement, self-esteem, *Self* magazine...self, self, self. However, growing up with Jane Fonda and Richard Simmons, Anthony Robbins and Stuart Smalley, *Donahue*, *Oprah*, Rikki Lake and Larry King, with child abuse, spouse abuse, sexual harassment, and drug abuse, with Dalkon Shields, asbestos, breast implants, and 1-800-LAWYERS, we have been bombarded by the commercialization of victim and wellness discourses (and surprisingly similar parodies) since we can remember.

The sheer volume of the discourse is persuasive, especially when you consider the fact that we have no point of contrast (for the most part, we only get to see sixties' communalism parodied by self-conscious Boomers embarrassed by their betrayal of the ideal). What is more, the discourse merely plays out metaphors for our own childhood experiences of personal responsibility.

ISOLATION DEFINES POST-MODERN LIFE

One needn't look far to find further evidence that Xers have been conditioned by the forces of post-modern atomization. More than any other generation, Xers use answering machines to screen calls, have food delivered, shop in catalogues, rent videos instead of going to the movies (and know how to operate the VCR—no "flashing 12:00" jokes here). Xers use television as a periscope on the outside world. We cannot wait for virtual reality.

Just as the general trends of suburbanization and the breakdown of institutional relationships diminish our sense of social connection, these specific examples of atomization, which continue to contextualize our life experience, have left Xers feeling isolated.

It is no wonder that Xers have grown up with such an acute sense of danger—of personal vulnerability. After all, we grew up on news of nuclear weapons, terrorism, serial killers and drive-by shootings, sex crimes in day care centers, guns in high school, date rape, *A Current Affair*, *sex, lies, and videotape*, *COPS*, police brutality, real urban riots, drug wars, and "Just Say No" feeling of safety.

Xers' puberty was greeted by AIDS, so we couldn't even enjoy the sexual revolution—another false promise of Boomerdom. As a result, Xers are comfortable with a certain feeling of detachment. If Holden Caulfield had been an Xer, he would have called a phone sex line at $2.95 a minute instead of getting punched in the face by a pimp in a sleazy hotel.

At the same time, the social structures that fueled Boomer rebellion had long disappeared. Xers didn't even have curfews in college—we had coed dorms, same-sex bathrooms, and nurse practitioners curing STDs in the university health center. "All you need is love" never worked for Xers...we have always had to use a condom.

All this contradiction leaves Xers with a strong sense of irony. It is our surest way of processing the lightning-fast complexity of post-modern life. But do not mistake our irony for cynicism. Irony—like healthy skepticism—is a tool for responding to the outside world. Cynicism is a tool for dealing with unpleasantness within yourself. Xers do not need cyncism. We are generally comfortable with ourselves.

XERS ARE USED TO SWIMMING AGAINST THE DEMOGRAPHIC CURRENT

By the time Xers were ready to go to work, everybody was going back home. Thirty-four million Americans are working out of home offices, companies are downsizing, pensions are portable, skills are increasingly specialized—the traditional workplace has all but disappeared. Safe jobs are scarce and Xers are entering the working world at the lowest rung of a very volatile job-ladder.

Xers' prospects for earning a reliable income are not secure. Unlike Boomers, whose fathers were the Organization Men who thrived in the post-World War II prosperity, our parents are not necessarily secure enough financially to stake us for very long if we fall on hard times. That means, yet again, we must look to ourselves for security.

I believe that what so many perceive in Xers as arrogance is actually a complex set of responses to a dangerous world in which we feel challenged to stake out a position of safety. Xers do not cower in the face of danger—we are used to taking care of ourselves. I think that the reason why Xers are so fiercely independent is the same reason Xers are such powerful innovators—taking care of ourselves, we have solved so many problems on our own and discovered so many original solutions that worked, Xers know in our hearts that there is always more than one way to peel an orange.

Creative ability is the most prized Xer trait.

"Allow Me The Space To Make Decisions"

This is the way I like to be managed: allow me the space to make decisions on my own, and to determine when and how I am going to do the work I need to do. I take responsibility for my work. I am accountable for the work I do. The more supervision there is, the more room I have to blame someone else, to say "if I had done it my way it would have turned out better, I was following orders, it turned out badly because of the way you told me to do it." I would care less about my work, put less into it and rely on others more to do what needs to be done. Instead, in my situation, I know what I need to do and when I need to do it and the buck stops here. To me that is everything. I respond when given responsibility.
Public interest lawyer

The Key Factor: "A Certain Level Of Trust"

It was good because his management style was very hands off and he left me alone to do my own thing.

Personally I react better to that. It is a certain level of trust that builds up. That, for me, makes me more motivated to work.
Staff consultant at an information systems consulting company

Real Quality Means A Whole Lot More

The more I am going to be able to have my ideas influencing what happens, that is going to make me happier, and generally that improves my work. If I am having more input, it is more likely that this is something that I am thinking about outside of work too. I am spending more time on it. If my ideas are being valued, then I am invested in the project and it means a whole lot more to turn out something of real quality.
Researcher in a public interest organization

"Let Me Fly With My Own Wings"

There is no greater boost in my job than when my manager says "I trust your judgment." I need someone who can be a coach and a mentor, who can give me the guidance I need, but let me fly with my own wings.
Assistant to the VP of human resources for a chemical manufacturing company

XERS WANT GOOD MANAGEMENT

What does this mean for managers? Managers must realize that, because Xers are used to solving problems on our own, we are natural innovators. As such, we hold tremendous potential value for any organization which understands how to foster Xers' innovation. If managers want to tap Xers' creative power, they need to honor Xers' independence instead of seeing that independence as a form of arrogance.

Managers who honor Xers' independence are able to motivate Xers' innovative drive by granting more day to day autonomy and enough creative responsibility to imagine problems in our own terms and deliver original solutions. The Xers who speak in this section make it clear that what so many perceive in Xers' as arrogance is really the expression of a strong desire to define problems, set priorities, make decisions, and even mistakes, develop innovative solutions, and produce great results on our own initiative.

Allowed this kind of entrepreneurial freedom, Xers are able to produce results in which we feel invested. We can learn and grow by doing, expand our abilities and believe we are making a mark on the organization. Most important, Xers and managers can see Xers' value reflected in the fruits of our innovation.

Good Managers Sit Down And Work Through Things

The good managers were the ones who would sit down and work through it with me and tell me, specifically, how to do a job better the next time. When a manager takes the time to show me specifically what I am doing right and wrong, then I can learn from him, and that makes me more focused on the work.

Associate at a management consulting firm

Making Mistakes Can Lead To Making A Difference

How do you motivate these people? Well, you have to give them responsibility, allow them some creative freedom, give them room to make decisions, to make mistakes, to feel like they are in a position to make a difference.

Associate administrator of a small hospital

XERS ARE NOT SLACKERS

There is no doubt that Xers are fiercely independent. We are used to solving problems solo. Xers are confident because our most poignant problem-solving successes have likely come in solitary efforts. We know our own track records and so we want to be taken seriously, trusted, and given responsibility. Xers want enough creative freedom to prove our abilities to managers and confirm our abilities to ourselves.

The kind of freedom Xers seek is a tangible creative space, defined less by square footage than by time. Creative space for Xers consists of an intervening time period between the making of assignments and their completion. That means assignments have to be well defined at the outset and Xers left alone in the interim.

"I Like To Control My Own Area"

The kind of manager I like is one who gives me an assignment and then leaves me alone to work on it on my own. I like to control my own area and worry about my own work and be left alone. A good manager should not be getting involved in the day to day work of his employees. The day to day work is what you have employees for.

Analyst at a major credit card company

Xers Have Fun Working Very Hard

I think a very entrepreneurial environment is a great atmosphere for me where I can have a lot of fun working very hard.

Vice president of a major investment bank

Satisfaction: Making Decisions That Affect The Bottom Line

I wanted to be working on my own side of a business. I like the experience of making decisions that affect the bottom line.

Marketing manager at a financial services company

XERS SEEK TRUST AND INVOLVEMENT

Xers' expressions of independence do not represent arrogance, but a desire to be personally invested in our work. Xers' personal investment is a function of the extent to which we have the opportunity to showcase our creative talents. That is why managers who give Xers creative autonomy benefit from our very best work.

Managers who convey trust and confidence in Xers' creative abilities inspire Xers to innovate. By gradually expanding Xers' scope of responsibility and the time frame between assignments and deadlines, managers create the space in which Xers are free to take risks and make mistakes—the only space in which innovation can occur.

"Let Me Figure Out A Way To Solve The Problem"

I like to have someone say to me, "I need a system to do this, what can you do to help me out," and then let me figure out a way to solve the problem. They say "here is a business problem that I have, how can you help me?" And I have to figure out a solution. That is the way I work best.

Analyst at a major credit card company

Room For A Lot Of Initiative

I have a lot of responsibility here and there is room for a lot of initiative. If I want to do something, I can go out on a limb. It is worth doing the extra here. I want to perform here.

Researcher for an investors' research service

Creative Strategies...That Aren't Obvious

My job, as I see it, is to come up with creative strategies and ways of doing things that are not necessarily obvious, so it is important that I have the latitude to try some things that might work and some things that might not work. That means I have to be left alone to try different approaches. Because if I only try the things that are tested I can only do what everyone else is doing. Because I am allowed that freedom, I am very innovative in my work.

Marketing coordinator for a publishing company

"My Product Is Who I Am and Says Everything About Me"

I stand alone, my work is me, my work product is who I am and says everything about me. I couldn't work without the creative freedom and the responsibility. I enjoy this style, which is giving me a lot of freedom to do my job, to do things my way.

Public interest lawyer

Monet And Rembrandt...It's All Great Art

Another teacher told me that he thought of his work as an art. "Some of us will paint in the style of Monet, some in the highly realistic style, some like Rembrandt, but it's all great art." Some teach with an extraordinary level of precision and clarity, some teachers are masters of the anecdote. That approach liberated me and others to bring our own styles into the classroom, to be ourselves. Whoever I am going to be as a teacher is going to be a unique expression of who I am. My work is going to be an expression of myself. I think it made me very daring in what I would do. I had enormous success as a teacher. I won the teacher of the year award, which was the first time a first year teacher had won the award. My experience was an enormous success because I approached my work as an art.

High school teacher

BOTTOM LINE: "TELL ME WHAT TO DO, GIVE ME INFORMATION, AND THEN LET ME CREATE!"

The secret to being a great teacher for Xers is emphasizing possibilities and options instead of necessary solutions. Xers don't want to learn that 2+2=4. Xers want to learn how to count and add, so that we can make 4 by adding 3+1 or 1+1+1+1. Information without unnecessary rules—that is what Xers crave.

Teaching Xers means giving Xers the resources to find original solutions to challenging problems, sharing information and methods of practice without dictating unnecessary rules, letting Xers learn by doing, and inspiring Xers to engage our innovative powers in the process. The devil is in the details. Sharing information means sharing the details, not just the motions. That takes time. It's worth it.

CHAPTER 3:

How Not To Manage Generation X

LEARNING FROM BAD EXPERIENCES

Some would say it is easy to point fingers—easier to decry the style and techniques of bad managers than to prescribe specific solutions to the challenge of managing Generation X. Solutions come later in this book, where I will share the stories of Xers being managed well. In this chapter, readers have the opportunity to learn from the mistakes of failed management relationships, from the managers who are bringing out the worst in Generation X.

This chapter is divided into four sections, based on the most common bad management syndromes shared by my interviewees: wasting time, micromanaging, fear based managing, and management without feedback. What these bad management syndromes have in common is that each attacks, in a different way, Xers' expression of individuality in our work and Xers' corresponding pursuit of self-building career security. The managers described in this chapter are imposing on Xers' time, space, and personal security. These managers make it hard for Xers' to make meaningful contributions, they undermine learning, diminish creative entrepreneurship, and make it impossible for Xers to monitor our investment at work.

The value of this chapter is not to be found in the chance to hate bad managers along with the Xers who describe them—there is no value in the negative emotions, per se. It is, rather, the chance to see up close what causes these negative emotions. For the Xers who speak in this chapter, it is an opportunity to explain the ways in which bad managers have a powerful impact on our attitudes and behavior. For managers, it is proof that your job is important—that there is a very real and concrete causal relationship between the behavior of managers and that of the managed.

The management practices highlighted in this chapter are uniquely intolerable to Xers. What is more, Xers react most viscerally to managers who impinge on our personal security, raising the costs of bad management and raising the stakes for managers who wish to improve the bottom line.

If Xers are searching, in our work, for opportunities to invest in ourselves, to build our portable proprietorships of ability, managers are searching for something in Xers' work, as well. Managers do not employ Xers merely because we are the next generation off the human resource conveyer belt. Managers and Xers have the same goal—for Xers to be valuable contributors in the workplace. In this chapter, Xers make a collective plea to managers to stop undermining that shared goal. For all those managers who have stomped off in anger, muttering under your breath, "What the hell is your problem?" Here is your answer.

WHEN MANAGERS MISUSE XERS' TIME

Considering the extent to which Xers have been portrayed as "slackers," readers may be surprised to read that the Xers whom I interviewed work fifty, sixty, seventy, and eighty hour weeks. Xers are not afraid of hard work—especially not the Star Xers who speak in this book. Still, many managers report that they find Xers recalcitrant when it comes to surrendering our schedules to managers. There is no question that Xers are willing to work long hard hours. Still, Xers are quite unwilling to have our time controlled by those who casually misuse such a valuable resource. Xers become frustrated and stymied when managers allow us no freedom to schedule the pursuit of our work goals. When managers insist on controlling our time and then waste it, Xers become resentful and bitter.

Remember that Xers are fiercely independent because we have had to fend so often for ourselves. From our school days as latchkey kids to our cool reception in the job market, Xers have trained ourselves on self-sufficiency. We prefer to work at our own pace. When managers deprive Xers of any ability to control our own schedules, they are striking at the core of our independence.

This is what causes Xers to become so protective of our time: managers who create false urgency because they fail to plan and managers who waste Xers' time. Xers are willing to devote our time to work, as long as managers respect that time as a mutual resource and recognize our need and ability to deploy it.

CHRONO-CRUNCH: SHORTAGE OF X-TIME RESULTING FROM BAD PLANNING, INEFFICIENCY OR LACK OF RESPECT

It's not easy to get ahead these days. But, Xers are

strong and ambitious. We are ready to use our time as a resource to succeed. Go ahead and challenge any of the Xers whom I interviewed to work a hundred-hour-week. Every one of them would enjoy a private chuckle and eagerly work side by side with any Boomer manager until he or she drops. We do hundred-hour-weeks—no problem.

Xers are on the front lines, putting in days on end, weekends, early mornings and late nights. For the vast majority of Xers with whom I spoke, a light week is fifty hours, an average week is sixty, and a brutal week is eighty to one hundred hours. That's a lot of hours.

Thirty-Eight Hours Straight—No Problem

The internship year is a blur, I was in the hospital 120 hours a week, minimum. One time, I had been working 38 hours straight with no breaks and I went to the operating room with one of the attending physicians. I hadn't shaved in two days, I was exhausted. The attending physician said to me "Can I give you two dollars?" I said "Why?" He said "So you can buy a razor." I said "I've been working for 38 hours straight. I haven't had any time to do anything, to shave, to pee, to eat, anything." He said "Why don't you take 15 minutes off to shave." So I did. Maybe it made me look more elegant.
Physician in first year internship

X TIME: SIXTEEN HOUR DAYS AND SEVEN DAY WEEKS, MISSED MEALS, SPINNING WHEELS, AND FOUR HOURS OF SLEEP

Xers Don't Hesitate To Stay Until 4:00 a.m.

Oh, staying until 4 a.m. every night in a week is the exception but not by as much as you'd think. The work is really demanding, it is a lot of hours, and the pay is

not that great. But, we are here to deliver the best and I'm just psyched to be part of it.
Assistant account executive at an advertising firm

Xers Work On Their Lap-Tops At The Hospital

I remember, one of the young analysts was in the hospital after an emergency appendectomy and his boss sent him a lap-top computer at the hospital with instructions to finish a financial model on which he had been working. It just gives you an idea of the priorities being applied there.
Associate at a small investment bank

Four Days Of Work Over The Weekend, "Have A Good Sunday"

You can't make anybody happy because everybody wants too much. Each senior VP on the way out the door on a Friday afternoon will give me a day's work for the weekend. The problem is there are four of them. Each of them says, "Here this is just one day's work, have a good Sunday." But four of them do that, so I have four days of work over the weekend. That means I cannot give anyone what they want, and I work the entire weekend and no one is happy. When I am overloaded like that, I can't get the satisfaction of doing a great job because I don't have time to put a bow on anything. It is difficult to produce the kind of quality I would want.
Vice president of a major investment bank

"I'm Here All Night Trying To Catch Up"

He is the kind of partner, and there are plenty of them, who will just call me up and say "come down to my office" and he will hang up before I can even say anything. Half the time he does this call on his speaker phone. I don't consider that the nicest way to request somebody's services. It's less polite. Whether or not I have something pressing to do, it is just expected that I will show up in his office within the next two minutes. And, of course, I have to drop my work no matter what I am in the middle of doing. That means I'm here all night trying to catch up on whatever he interrupts during the day.

Associate at a big law firm

HOW BAD PLANNING CAUSES FALSE URGENCY

Managers who fail to plan Xers' time effectively are diminishing the value of a potentially precious resource. The Xers who speak in this section describe managers who insist on maintaining close control over Xers' time at work, but fail to create operative work schedules so that Xers' work goals can be coordinated with our managers' requirements. Xers told me about managers who hold onto deadlines until the last minute, making Xers wait around all day and run around all night; managers who seem to have glue on their desks and can't keep up with Xers' fast paced productivity; managers who routinely under-staff projects so that everyone is frantic until the cavalry gets pulled off their horses and thrown in to fill the gaps in the battle line.

When managers insist on controlling Xers' time and do a poor job maximizing it, they confirm Xers' pre-judgment that we are much better able than managers to schedule our time effectively. What is more, Xers become increasingly vigilant about guarding our time from such managers. The managers described in the following section would have a hard time disputing that pre-judgment and would be better off if they included Xers in the management of our own time.

A Task I Normally Enjoy Giving A Lot Of Time

Work becomes stressful when I set a pace for my day and goals for my day and then all of a sudden I have to set all that aside and before I know it I am working under my manager's sudden time pressure. It is always ASAP, always "I need this yesterday." If my time management is good but my manager's time management is bad, I am still the one who pays the price. Things that could have been planned were not. It is really a time management issue. When my responsibilities are all mixed up with my manager's schedule, because he is so much less efficient, I have to race through work that should get more time. In that situation I am always running the risk of doing a less good job. It certainly makes my work less enjoyable. It could be a task that I would normally enjoy giving a lot of time, but it gets put in this pressurized environment.

Marketing executive for commercial manufacturer

Poor Planning Diminishes The Value Of X-Time

Management there is non-existent. It's a fire-drill mentality. Nothing is done until the last minute and then it has to be done immediately. The worst thing is the lack of planning on our end. I could work 8 a.m. to 11 p.m. and that would be fine. The problem is we spend a bunch of time during the day doing nothing or next to nothing, because our manager doesn't get to the point where he has work for us. Once the manager gets to that point and has an assignment, all of a sudden it is urgent, there is no time even for adequate instructions. All of a sudden, I am looking at being at work all night, after waiting around all day doing nothing. It means I have no life, can't make any plans, ever. It wouldn't bother me so much except that a little planning would make it possible to do a lot of the work during the day that gets done in

the middle of the night.
Associate in an investment bank

"There Was No Need To Create Such Urgency"

What most people resent is when a partner will know of a deadline days or weeks or even months before it occurs and then doesn't get around to delegating the work until the last minute. That means that all of a sudden an associate has to stay until all hours, maybe around the clock, when there was really no need to create such an urgency. Of course, it makes people a lot less interested in working for those partners and it makes people resentful of the work that they have to do for them.
Associate at a big law firm

MANAGERS WHO CAN'T MANAGE X-TIME EFFECTIVELY SHOULD LET XERS MANAGE OUR OWN TIME

Beware Of Bottle Necks At Word Processing

The time catch is that word processing decides what work gets done based on urgency, not based on the order in which they receive the job. No matter what time I might get my work to word processing, my work will sit in word processing for a day. So then I am stuck. Any deadline for another project will throw me off the top of the line. And there are lots of them. If I am a week ahead, I might as well forget my project because it is going to sit around for a week, until it is urgent. I have no control over it at all. Then the night before my own deadline, we are leaning on word processing and holding up everyone else. It was more a lack of management than bad management.
Associate in an investment bank

Xers Want To Use Time Efficiently And Produce...But Managers' Turn-Around Time Slows Us Down

With one of my senior editors I feel he holds up my work. He takes four days to decide to read something I give him and when he gives it back to me, I might have a whole day's work to revise it. If he could turn his part around faster, I could have more comfort with my own deadlines.

Associate editor of a newsstand magazine

"I Felt Like He Held All The Cards"

The biggest problem was that we were clearly dependent on our manager to keep the project moving. We had all this data and it was just a matter of compiling it—that was the time consuming part. We waited a lot of the time for our manager to catch up with us and give us more data to work with. I felt like he kind of held all the cards, in terms of the speed at which this thing was produced. It seemed to prolong the project, because we kept missing deadlines.

Researcher in an investment information service

...Yanked Off Of One Project And Thrown Onto Another

Management began taking people from their projects and throwing them on the tail end of another project which was in urgent need. That meant there were people who were always being thrown onto the end of something, instead of having a full team staffed on a project from beginning to end. Instead of looking for the best team for a project, they were filling in gaps. It is very disconcerting to be yanked off of one project and just thrown onto another. For one thing it is disorienting. For another thing, there is this period of time, maybe two months, where you are absent from the project you were working on. Plus, whenever that happened to me it sort of made

me question how important the original project was that I got yanked away from. When that becomes routine, there seems to be a developing imbalance between the hardship and any kind of gains. I certainly wasn't putting in extra hours and all kinds of extra effort when it became clear that none of my needs and wants were being included. It is also hard to feel like I am on a career path when I have no control over what I am working on and have no way to direct my own goals.
Engineer

HOW MANAGERS MISUSE X-TIME

Xers guard our schedules most jealously against managers who are capricious about wasting our time. We don't mind working long hard hours, but we are very reluctant to work long unproductive hours. The Xers who speak in this section describe managers who are shameless about wasting X-time, including managers who keep Xers around late so they can justify inflating fees based on billable hours—a fact that clients are loathe to hear. But, it's not all about billing. A lot of Xers told me about "face time," hanging around the office late hours just so managers can see them "working" late because the corporate culture frowns on leaving early.

Equally dreaded are gopher weekends at the hands of managers who still don't know how to operate the photocopier and the fax machine. Finally, some managers are just inconsiderate: You'll read about a senior partner at a law firm who managed to waste thirty-six hours of X-time in one short hour and a half.

He Would Not Let Us Leave, Even Though We Didn't Have Work

This manager was padding our hours by taking extra time

after we were done at say 9 p.m. to do whatever it was. He would not let us leave, even though we didn't have work at that point. He would make us stay, so we would have to bill the hours.
Consultant at a big six accounting firm

DON'T WASTE EMPHASIS ON FACE TIME—IT'S AN OUT-MODED CONCEPT

Neither Xers Nor Clients Approve Of Overbilling

There was a lot of face time. The staffing manager would walk around at 11 p.m. every night and if you weren't there, you got a new project the next day. I got home before 10 p.m. twice all year but the company wasn't that busy which made these expectations ludicrous. The VP would leave at 11 p.m., the associates at 11:05, and the analysts at 11:10. On my second to last day, I left at 8 p.m. and I got yelled at the next day. What you have to realize is that we weren't even billing hours. So why the focus on hours? It was quantity versus quality. When the only way to differentiate your work is by the number of hours you are working, that is comical. There was nobody in the firm who was managing the business, making it a good place to work or a valuable experience. I found it frustrating and felt they were wasting a lot of my time. So I left.
Analyst at an investment bank

"I Didn't Want To Be There Just To Send Out Faxes"

We had one manager who asked to have us in a lot of extra hours and weekends, even if it wasn't really necessary. He just liked to have support staff around to do his faxing, typing, copying. He preferred relying on other people to do his running around. I didn't like having to go in when I wasn't really needed. I am glad to put in

extra time, but not when it is unnecessary. It really affected my attitude toward him because I hated being there just to send out faxes and make copies.
Staff assistant in a subcommittee of the United States Congress

Twenty-four Attorneys Sitting On A Bus For An Hour And A Half

Everyone had to travel by bus to attend a recruiting event. The law firm did a memo telling people that if they were going to attend the event, they had to be on the bus on time. Everybody was on the bus at the appointed time with the exception of one senior partner. Twenty-four young attorneys and myself ended up sitting on that bus for an hour and a half waiting for this senior partner who just couldn't manage to fulfill that time commitment. He knew the bus would wait for him. You can't tell me that what this guy was doing was worth wasting everyone else's time.
Recruiting manager for a mid-sized law firm

NO SPACE—WHEN MANAGERS MICRO-MANAGE XERS

It is the buzzword of all managers and management consultants: "micro-management." Most would agree it is a style to be avoided. For Xers, it is anathema. If it feels intangible, let my interviewees explain just how simple it is.

How do you know if you are micro-managing? If you are giving people discreet one-hour assignments and they have to keep coming back to you over and over again for each little assignment, that means you are micro-managing them.

When Xers reach for greater independence and creative freedom in our work, we are not expressing arrogance or insolence. Xers' desire for more responsibility and room to create in our work is an expression of our entrepreneurism and innovative spirit, natural extensions of our self-nurtured independence.

If managers want to maximize Xers' productivity, they would be wise to encourage our natural predispositions and help Xers to be entrepreneurial with management driven work goals. However, a great many managers do just the opposite: they insist on controlling Xers' every movement, attempting to squelch our creative impulses, and denying us any responsibility for tangible end-products.

The managers described in this section are cramping Xers' style. Xers told me about managers who can't keep their hands off Xers' work, involving themselves in the most mundane tasks, insisting on round after round of changes, taking an hour to finalize a routine letter, four years to put out a newsletter, looking over shoulders, nitpicking details, second-guessing results and halting final products with one last suggestion, and maybe one more, and maybe "this is the last change, I promise."

Micro-managers spend so much time intertwined with Xers that no one has time to do any work. Managers cannot devote sufficient time to senior level work when they are focused on lower level tasks that belong in the hands of Xers, while Xers cannot deliver results with managers attached at the hip. What is more, denying Xers any responsibility for tangible end-products means that we have no room to innovate. The consequence of micro-management is that the hard work of two or more potentially effective people is reduced to the productivity-level of one ineffective person.

For Xers, micro-management is a devastating motivation killer.

MICRO-MANAGERS CAN'T LET GO OF XERS' WORK BECAUSE THEY DON'T TRUST THEMSELVES

Instead of encouraging our natural predisposition to be innovative and entrepreneurial, micro-managers disenfranchise Xers from the results of our work. Robbed of any ownership or ability to affect the end-products of our work, Xers are a wasted resource at best. In the worst cases, Xers who are micro-managed become angry, disaffected and counterproductive—and then we leave.

A Familiar Scene: The Manager Who Can't Let Go

When my manager controls my every movement and won't let go of my work for even a minute, it isn't long before I stop caring altogether about the whole thing. I tend to do exactly what I need to do to get by and hide in the men's room the rest of the time. It gets ridiculous when my manager controls my transmittal letters to the point of changing "very truly yours" to "sincerely." I mean, come on. It just doesn't seem to matter anymore.
Analyst at an investment bank

"Hands All Over Everything"

My manager would have his hands all over everything. He would ask me to do something—a letter, for instance. I would do it and he would have corrections or additions. But that process would keep happening several times. He would keep changing his mind, want more words changed. We would spend an hour getting out a routine letter—less than three quarters of a page. Once, we were putting together a binder for a trade show. It was a pretty straightforward thing, lists of names and times and some other information. Anyone with a bit of initiative and a little common sense could put together a fine product that would far exceed what was necessary. But, this manager just couldn't really bring himself to delegate anything. Even with this, he ultimately did it himself and took twice as much time by involving me in it. Involving me in routine tasks like a letter or putting together a notebook of information is supposed to save my manager valuable time. But, because he couldn't even delegate the most minor things, it became counter-productive to even have me involved because we would just go back and forth on everything.

Staffer for a trade association of manufacturers

"He Thinks That No One Else In The World Is Competent"

The main problem that I am confronting is that the manager is very hesitant to let go and he is so over controlling. It has been very frustrating, because he is the classic self-made entrepreneur and he thinks that no one else in the world is competent. Let me give you an example. There should have been a national newsletter every three months for the organization. But, the last one was put out four years ago. Why? Because the last communications director wasn't allowed to ever put anything out. He was edited to death by my manager. Finally, we hired some very capable people to help put out a newsletter. They produced a newsletter, which was very good, and they did it in no time. My manager has re-written it completely seven times and it still isn't going out, nor is there any set date for it. I want to tell my manager that he is making a fool out of me out there, because we haven't met the deadlines which we set.

Executive staff of a non-profit foundation

"She Wouldn't Believe Until She Tried It Herself"

If an experiment didn't work, my research director wouldn't believe that the experiment wouldn't work until she tried it herself. So I would spend weeks trying to do an experiment and come to her to explain that it would not work. Finally she would get mad and try it herself. Then, of course, she would say "you were right, it didn't work." One time, after a situation like this, I heard her saying to a bunch of people that she didn't believe a word I was saying until she tried the experiment herself. Why have me there at all?

Research scientist at a major research university

MICRO-MANAGING ISN'T REALLY MANAGING AT ALL

What makes micro-managing the least effective, least efficient and most time consuming management approach?

Micro-managing isn't really managing at all. Managing people is about defining tasks and appropriate spheres of responsibility so as to facilitate their maximal productivity. But, this is precisely what micro-managers fail to do. They are unable to map out the appropriate boundaries between their own work goals and the work goals of the people they manage. Some of the Xers who speak in this section attribute this failure to the arrogance of managers—to their conviction that only they can be trusted to complete the work at hand. However, most Xers perceive, in micro-managers' inability to trust others, that micro-managers lack confidence in their own ability to manage effectively. They are always chasing after the work product to double and triple check it and change it again and again. As a consequence, the end-products resulting from their management are always their own. This puts an unfortunate cap on productivity.

But, for Xers, the damage is greater than diminished productivity. For Xers, who are committed to creating our own end-products, it is difficult to be committed to a creative process in which even the most trivial results will never bear our imprint. Where end-results are not likely to contain any of the work we produce, there is little reason to be productive.

Missing The Concepts In Search Of Typos

My manager has difficulty delegating and developing trust in the people who are working for him. In anything that really matters, he is totally involved with it and has his hands all over it. The weird thing is that he tends to focus in on spelling mistakes and typos instead of being a more visionary type guy. That makes you kind of wonder about his ultimate value to the company. If I know that my manager is going to go over every detail, rewrite every word on the page, that provides me with a huge disincentive to do a good job, to really do the best job that I can do. Why? Because I know that it really doesn't matter, because the manager is going to make the thing his own and totally rewrite it, no matter how good of a job I do. So, why should I put in the effort at all? The manager might as well do the whole thing on his own. Of course, the contrast is with a manager who from the start conveys that a piece of work is going to be my responsibility. That if I don't do a great job, there is not going to be anybody covering my back. It's me or no one. That is the best incentive to do a good job because I know the whole thing is riding on me. If a manager conveys to me that he doesn't trust my work, why the hell should I work hard for him? I'm not saying that there should be no quality check. But let me take a stab at it. I don't mind failing and learning from that if I can have a chance to do a good job and have it matter.

Business development associate in a major entertainment and theme park company

THE MICRO-MANAGER IS ALWAYS LOOKING FOR A MISTAKE, EVEN IF HE HAS TO CREATE ONE

Causing Needless Strain In Work Relationships

Some things don't need to go through the bureaucracy and analysis and multiple hurdles. It often feels like my manager throws up hurdles for no reason other than to say, "ha, gotcha!" Even like a vacation day: if she is going to say "yes," say "yes." Don't haggle over it. I have to sit down with her and kind of dance with her over every little thing. She is gone from the office a lot. Her absence is the main source of my autonomy, which is also when I am able to meet my work objectives best. It is hard to work with her looking over my shoulder. If it weren't for this strain on our relationship, I would be able to do a lot more and be happier with it. I am looking for employment elsewhere.

Marketing specialist for a heavy equipment manufacturer

NOBODY EVER HELD OUR HANDS BEFORE—XERS DON'T NEED MANAGERS TYING OUR HANDS AT WORK

Try Not To Stop Projects Already In Motion

This manager has been very much in my face. He is continually giving unsolicited criticism, halting projects that are already in motion, nitpicking details, and he is affecting my productivity. Several times projects were already completed and approved by the executive director and then this manager would come back with a bunch of suggestions and insist that things be done his way. I felt halted in my tracks and that this guy wanted control over everything I was doing. He was affecting the morale and productivity in the office.

Admissions director for a non-profit educational organization

"I Can't Baby-Sit Every Piece Of Paper"

My manager wants me following him around doing every little thing for him like I'm attached to him. He gets a call and says to me "Where is this piece of paper or that?" or "I need such and such right now to talk on the phone." I want to say "I can't baby-sit every piece of paper that you deal with." He will snap and get mad because I can't instantly turn up every piece of paper that he needs the moment he needs it. I have no space to do my own work because my manager is practically attached at my hip.

Account coordinator in an advertising firm

Chronic Second Guessing Is Primarily Stupid

My experience with this manager was miserable because he tried to micro-manage every little piece of my work. It was hard for him to imagine that each member of the design team was more knowledgeable about our own particular area of expertise than he was. He continually second guessed all of our work. Obviously I am going to work a lot less hard on that kind of work than I would on work where I have a lot of input. It was so bad that I decided to look for another job. In the end that manager was demoted and then later fired.

Electrical engineer

RULE OF X: ANYONE YOU ABUSE HAS A POWERFUL INCENTIVE TO UNDERMINE YOUR AUTHORITY

Most people would be surprised to hear the stories of abuse in the workplace which Xers tell in this section. Too many of the Xers I interviewed told me about managers blowing up at employees, having temper tantrums in the office, actually yelling and screaming at Xers, calling Xers names, throwing things at us, putting us down, humiliating Xers, and generally managing us by pushing us around.

Managers are blowing off a lot of steam at work and Xers are taking a lot of heat.

Then again, maybe these stories would *not* come as such a surprise.

The ethos of anger, fear, and intimidation is killing morale in offices all over America. Because Xers are the newest employees in the workplace, we suffer disproportionately from management abuse. Managers who either cannot or will not control their tempers are abusing the Xers who work for them.

How do abused Xers react? Like others who are abused in the workplace, we learn to hate our managers and to hate our jobs with the deepest contempt imaginable. We spend way too much time and energy ducking for cover and looking for a way out, wading in bruised egos, hurt feelings, vicious gossip and high turnover. Before we leave abusive work situations, however, abused Xers begin singing contempt— building the cynical chorus in the workplace which drives morale through the floor.

But, remember, Xers are not alone with our pain—Xers have each other and we have a lot of information with which to interpret abuse in the workplace and shape more complex responses. Xers are a well educated work force. What is more, we are thinkers and we are talkers.

More important, Xers were raised amidst the discourses of wellness and victimization floating over the satellite beams and airways and pages and conversations. The victim and wellness models, which surround all Americans today, were shaped by the same forces which shaped Xers' childhood.

Having grown up in a world determined by the dangers of post-modern life and feeling a sense of great personal vulnerability, Xers are particularly sensitive to personal danger. We know abusive relationships pose a danger to our well being.

ABUSIVE MANAGERS ARE JUST LIKE ALL ABUSERS

Xers interpret abusive managers in much the same context as we have learned to interpret what we know about other abusers—abusive spouses, parents, teachers, clergy. Xers assume that managers' abusive behavior has more to do with their own psychological issues than it has to do with Xers' actual work performance.

The Xers who speak in this section describe abusive managers' wrathful tempers with a familiar pop-psyche spin: "non-people-persons," "school-yard bully syndromes," "abusive family situations," "painful childhoods," "venting frustrations," "a lot of anger," "problems with women," "problems expressing anger," "power complexes," "abusive attitudes," "control issues," "mood swings," and "stressing out."

Xers know that our abusive managers share a problem—and the problem is with themselves, not with us. We observe behavior in abusive managers which is obviously psychologically dysfunctional, in a category close to that of spouse abusers and child abusers and all the rest made famous by popular culture. Whatever personal issues abusive managers need to resolve, they need to find venues for working out their psychological dysfunctions without attacking the people who work for them. Until they stop attacking Xers, abusive managers will continue hurting the people they manage—and hurting company profits. They also expose their companies and themselves to huge liabilities from potential discrimination and hostile work environment lawsuits.

But you don't have to write off managers who are having difficulty. Generational miscues can create genuine management problems—worth solving like any other. Senior managers should devote as much attention to working through these problems as they do to other cultural or social issues in the workplace.

"I Never Know When He Is Going To Blow Up"

My manager's temper makes me a little worried about each piece of work I do. I think to myself, "is this bullet proof?" My manager is very demanding and is a non-people-person. Even though I think he has a very good side to him, it is not apparent to the untrained eye. It's not exactly a tantrum, but he can have a very bad temper and get very angry. It makes me nervous at work because I don't know when he is going to blow up.
Head of circulation for a magazine holding company

Staff Management By Jekyll And Hyde

My manager will be incredibly charming one minute and then, maybe, totally blast his secretary right in front of me. Say, in the middle of a sentence to me that is very sweet and controlled, he will stick out his head and yell at his secretary in a really nasty way. This is like a technique where he shows his capacity for anger. It is very intimidating. His power derives from the fact that people are afraid of him, like a schoolyard bully syndrome. He is liable to jump down my throat for the smallest failure.
Senior staffer in a non-profit foundation

"It Was Like An Abusive Family Situation"

The manager developed a pattern where he would yell at people and get them scared sh#tless of him and then smooth it over, once they were scared of him. He would go nuclear, yell at us, kick us out of his office, come around and yell at us individually. Then, ten minutes later, he would come out smiling and chatting as if nothing happened. It was a little like an abusive family situation. The people who stayed there would complain like crazy one day and then the next day, they would say "he's not so bad." Like abused children, they would find fault with themselves or with extraneous situations, so as not to have to blame the manager. On the other hand, I thought the guy was such an ass that I loved watching him screw up.

Cable television network employee

"She Even Yanked Me Around By The Arm"

If I made a little mistake, she would say "you lied to me" or call me "a little sh#t." She even yanked me around by the arm, physically, a couple of times. She threw stuff at me a couple of times. It was a general mental attitude that was belligerent and abusive. Sometimes she wouldn't let us take meals—she would make us work through meals. It was pretty crazy. I was hungry, my body was falling apart. We were working these crazy hours. She would just keep rattling things off. Everything is an emergency. I have been successful in my life and am used to good feedback which made this whole experience totally demoralizing. The thing is, to do this job well requires a lot of initiative. But, I was definitely in cover-your-ass mode. Doing the right thing might generate a backlash or cause some control issue. So it totally cut down on my initiative. It was very much a rule by fear atmosphere. I wasn't free to kick around ideas. I would follow instructions to the letter without taking any initiative. It wears you down. I started to get a bitter attitude toward this manager. There was so much friction that it was impossible to communicate. Then it is just that much harder to do a good job.

Consultant at a big six accounting firm

CRUELTY IS MUCH MORE COSTLY THAN KINDNESS
A Style Is So Cruel That It Crushes Morale

This manager is extremely controlling in a really sick and twisted way. Maybe she had a 'painful childhood.' She looks for things to be wrong, like staples instead of paperclips or the other way around or whatever. Basically I am always just waiting for her to chew me out. Her style is so cruel that morale is really low. It makes you feel like a bull in a China shop. Making mistakes that would seem small to anyone else, in our small world, are pretty grave. Everyone here can tell you how they learned to do something "right" by getting "burned" for doing it wrong. People are really tired of it and they are out of here like there is a revolving door. We have been working on an ongoing project for two years already, which has at least another year to go. There is a big learning curve, so it is very costly to have high turnover.
Information systems manager in a consumer goods company

Teeth-Grinding As Motivation

If I screw up someone is bound to say, "grrr, grrr." They vent their frustrations. The horrible feeling is that I feel trapped. Is it the kind of thing that motivates me to do my best? I have to do my best just to get out of here, just to not get yelled at—I have to do my best under the circumstances.
Analyst at an investment bank

CAPRICIOUS ANGER UNDERMINES ANY OTHER FAIR SYSTEM OF EVALUATION
I Am Going To Get Screwed No Matter How Good It Is

He had real mood swings. At 10 a.m., he could be your

best buddy and then at 10:30 he could be chewing you out. It made me always brace myself for the worst. I would think, "OK, if he is in a good mood, this piece of work is totally fine, if he is in a bad mood, then I am going to get screwed no matter how good it is." It was a case where I had to always be ready for the worst case and I would just hope that the screaming wouldn't be as bad as normal. At first it makes you try to do more work, because you are like preparing for the worst and trying to do extra to avoid getting yelled at. After a while, you get a learned helplessness. I would feel that whether it is good or bad I am going to get screwed so why should I put my all into it. That is a dangerous and degenerative attitude to have and of course it brings work quality way down.

Staff person in a political office

Managers with volatile tempers keep Xers in a state of fear, which is the greatest motivational dead-end. Xers seek to learn from managers' feedback. However, it is impossible to learn from irrational outbursts because they are not connected to reliable predictors. Thus, abusive managers make it impossible for Xers to learn to improve our performance.

Xers are not afraid of abusive managers, per se. That is, the actual consequences of authority are no more pernicious at the hands of abusive managers. What causes fear in Xers is the unpredictability which makes it impossible to prepare and condition our behavior to accommodate our managers' authority.

LIKE DRIVING ON A CRAZY HIGHWAY

In an environment of rational consequences, it is possible to condition your behavior. Driving on a highway with a speed limit of 55 miles per hour and a minimum speed of 45 miles per hour, you can make intelligent decisions about how fast to drive. You might decide to drive 60 m.p.h., despite the rules, because you have learned that the highway police only stop cars going 65 m.p.h. or more. Now imagine the same highway, with no speed limit and a patrolman who pulls over cars indiscriminately.

Of course, maybe the patrolman feels there is an organizing rationality to his approach even though no one else can figure it out, or maybe he pulls over cars whenever he is feeling personal anxiety about driving the patrol car, or maybe he pulls over cars whenever he is in a bad mood. How fast do you drive? Probably, you try not to drive at all, or at least not when that patrolman is around. Maybe you look for an alternative route.

Fear motivates avoidance and paralysis. What Xers learn in an environment of fear is that we are unwilling to indulge our managers' self-indulgence. Rather, we hide out until we can find an alternative route.

"People Don't Have Time To Be Polite"
You get beaten down all day long. People are physically beaten by being kept up all the time and then verbally dressed down periodically which is even more exhausting. There is very little encouragement. If something goes wrong, you are going to hear about it. There is a lot of anger. People feel they don't have time to be polite.
Associate at a major investment bank

MANAGERS NEVER SAVE TIME BY FOSTERING ANGER AND RESENTMENT
He Was So Mean That I Had To Take Most Of A Day Off
If we disagreed about anything, my manager would walk

away from me angry and shaking his head—and then he wouldn't speak to me for a while. This guy just didn't know how to express his anger in a positive way and it is very hard to function when someone is being mean. It really affected me. One time, he was so mean to me that I felt sick and had to take most of a day off. I also started losing a lot of weight and I was running all the time. Just because of all the pressure, I was going on these great long runs. I did get in great shape. The whole time I was doing stupid things at work and having a hard time getting along with people at the office. All of my positive energy went into running and none of it went into the office.

Office manager for a Washington based policy group

AND MANAGERS DIMINISH THEIR OWN POWER WHEN THEY TEAR DOWN THE PEOPLE THEY MANAGE

Treating People Badly To Make Themselves Feel Powerful

There are a lot of people in positions of authority who treat people abusively and make themselves feel better by exercising their power in that explicit manner. They have this power complex and they treat people like sh#t to make themselves feel powerful. The work I do involves skipping meals and not being able to go to the bathroom during meetings.

Associate at an investment bank

"...The Way No One Should Ever Yell At Anyone"

She yelled at me the way no one should ever yell at anybody and for really stupid things. There was something the matter with her. If something went wrong or if I did something not exactly the way she wanted, she would yell and scream, "How could you do that? You should know that. How could you not know this?" Always for something that was really a matter of opinion or that there was no way I could know. I would have tears in my eyes because she would make me feel like I had done these terrible, awful things, when really they were just stupid little things. One time we were having a conference call and my manager turns to me and says, "Do you have that mini tape recorder? Can you bring it down?" The conference call had already started. I went really fast, grabbed the tape recorder and I even had blank tapes. I brought it right back down to her. She asked if I had tested the tape recorder. I started to say I had tested the batteries and she completely freaked out and started yelling and screaming at me. I just thought to myself, "Wow, the tape recorder is fine, but she should get her batteries tested."

Assistant account executive at an advertising agency

ABUSIVE MANAGERS INSPIRE WHISPERING OFFICE REBELLIONS

He Would Reduce His Staff To Tears

It was a small office, absolutely dominated by the CEO, who was an extremely difficult person. He was impossible to please, a real screamer. This man was so impatient that he would reduce his staff to tears on a regular basis. The guy was in his mid fifties, unmarried, and his entire staff consisted of women under the age of 30. He was so mean, impatient, intimidating. I think that it was a purposeful thing on his part—he has some problems with women. I think he found it easier to push women around. He would yell at the top of his lungs if someone couldn't find a phone number. He would fly off the handle over the littlest things. I spent a lot of energy trying to avoid him. I would arrange my lunch hour so as to avoid him. I would arrange to leave the office when I

*knew he would be there and be there when I knew he
was going to be out. I just didn't like going in to work.
Everyone recognized the problem and banded together
privately in quiet rebellion. People quit regularly too.*
**Assistant public affairs coordinator for a public interest
media firm**

WHEN XERS NEED TO CREATE PERSONAL SUPPORT NETWORKS FOR ABUSED COWORKERS, XERS' ENERGIES ARE DISTRACTED FROM MANAGEMENT GOALS

Like others who are abused, Xers in abusive management relationships experience emotional and physical exhaus-
tion. Beyond the feelings of low morale and demotivation
inspired by abusive managers, abused Xers suffer from
depression and even from physical illness. Not only do these
effects raise employers' costs related to sick-time and medical care, they cause Xers to galvanize around the issue of
well-being for ourselves and for our peers.

On an individual basis, abused Xers withdraw into
ourselves in search of non-work related self-building strategies to pursue until we find new jobs. Among our peers,
abused Xers will defy the ethos of fear and intimidation,
converting the workplace into an environment of growth and
rational feedback by building support networks among ourselves.

Where managers make it impossible for us to learn and
grow through our work, Xers work together through our
shared experience to enhance a different kind of skill repertoire—our repertoire for coping with and avoiding and exacting revenge on abusive managers.

Because we divert so much creative energy to this group
effort, Xers are dangerous as office rebels. We incite subtle

forms of rebellion which can affect the bottom line dramatically.

The Office Grapevine Flourishes In Managerial Manure

You would hear someone getting totally abused by the Congressman, like getting yelled at in a dehumanizing personal way, being called a "sh#t," or a "f#cking idiot," right where everyone could hear it. The second that person came out of the Congressman's office, everyone would talk it out with the person. Like, "The Congressman is just out of control today" or "He is just a big asshole" or, "Hey, is there something I can do to help?" When you work for someone who is really abusive and in such a small office, everyone has to really stand by and support each other.

Legislative assistant in a busy congressional office

UNDERMINING XERS' SELF-CONFIDENCE IS THE FASTEST WAY TO KILL XERS' MOTIVATION

He Would Make Me Feel Like A Piece Of Dirt

He can really cut you down and make you feel like a complete idiot. Once when I was asking him a question...he must have been stressed out for some reason. He just snapped at me and said "just do it" in a really snide tone of voice. A couple of times he has said things that made me so furious that I wanted to cry—it really made me feel like a piece of dirt. The only thing I could do was walk back to my office. The way some of them treat associates makes me wonder about their upbringing, whether they were always such rude and inconsiderate people or whether being in this law firm for so many years has made them this way. The way we are treated is surprising because here we are lawyers and you would think, somehow, people could treat each other with some level of respect and decency. That goes out the door when there is any pressure. Some of them have the reputation of having screaming fits, which is surprising to me, considering the amount of education and training they have had to go through to get to where they are.

Associate at a big law firm

MANAGERS LOSE XERS' RESPECT WHEN WE SEE MANAGERS ABUSING OUR PEERS

Conferenced In From His Sick Bed

One time this partner called a team meeting and conferenced-in an associate who had been working really hard and was home very sick with the flu. In the middle of the conference call, in front of a room full of this guy's colleagues, this partner says, "I know you're not really sick, what are you doing home?" Then, in the middle of the meeting he stops and says to this poor sick guy, "What did I just say?" He berated the guy for not paying attention and then in a sarcastic voice he said, "I know you are very sick," and hung up the phone without even saying "goodbye." This was just a typical example of the way a lot of the partners behave toward associates in the firm. For some reason, they feel a need to treat the associates in this degrading manner.

Associate at a big law firm

ABUSIVE MANAGERS ARE THE TARGETS OF E-MAIL CHARACTER ASSASSINATION: HIGH TECH WATER COOLER SNICKERING

"Her Staff Had Been Sending Nasty E-Mail Messages"

There is one manager in our company who comes up every day in conversation. She has a weird power com-

plex—her thing seems to be to completely destroy people and then try to lure them back with a little bit of civility. The people who work for her hate her guts. One time recently this manager did an E-Mail survey and she found out that all of the people who worked for her had been sending really offensive messages about how much they hated her, about how psycho she was, and what a bitch she was, and all kinds of lewd offensive stuff about her. She went berserk of course.

Business development executive at a cable television network

GIVEN THE CHANCE, XERS WILL EXACT SWEET REVENGE

Revenge On The Basketball Court

The second day we were there, the manager on the project stormed in and kind of read us the riot act. This guy was screaming and yelling at us about how we had better produce for him, that he would be watching us, that he wouldn't take any sh#t from us. He turned out to be the project ogre—probably has hemorrhoids. You couldn't look cross-eyed at this guy without him jumping down your throat. When we all got together and played basketball one time, this guy was on the other team. It was like our big opportunity. Before, during and after the game, we were all talking about how we wanted to beat the sh#t out of this guy on the basketball court. He was a marked man. It was hilarious. This guy didn't get any easy buckets, that's for sure. Any time he even looked at the basket he had a forearm across his back or over his arm. He was getting chopped all over the place. We still talk about that one.

Program analyst

THE BEST WAY TO DEMOTIVATE XERS IS TO MAKE US FEEL THAT WE ARE NOT GETTING THE REWARDS WE DESERVE

Managers who complain that Xers are unwilling to pay dues are misinterpreting Xers' impatience for short-term rewards and indications of success. Dues paying is a problematic concept for Xers who can expect little in the way of long-term security in any sphere of our lives. From employers we cannot expect job security in the form of lifelong employment. From the world, we expect minimal future stability with respect to environmental and economic conditions, as well as basic family and social structures.

Indeed, Xers are ambitious for short-term rewards and indications of success—we learned to be this way in a short-term world. Xers' ambition is, in fact, a quest for security in the face of a world governed by instability.

While Xers know we cannot find the old fashioned job security in employment relationships, we seek, in our work and careers, a new form of security to provide the firm ground lacking in every other sphere of life.

For Xers, our work and careers represent potentially invaluable sources of personal security because Xers have learned to regard our work-repertoires and creative abilities as the primary tool-kit for navigating through the challenges in our lives.

The reason that Xers are so eager for immediate rewards from managers is that short-term indications of success in our work provide Xers with evidence that our tool-kits are still effective. Short-term rewards confirm for Xers that we are not wasting our time—that our investment of time and creative energy is being appropriately valued by managers.

The Xers who speak in this section told me about managers who fail to offer Xers any regular confirmation that our hard work is paying off. The managers in this section insist on withholding from Xers any indications of success and, as a result, they undermine Xers' ability to find personal security through our work. Managers who offer Xers no recognition, no thanks, no credit, no reward, in many cases no feedback of any kind, make it impossible for Xers to monitor the value of contributing our hard work.

A Simple "Thank You?"

Is it really so unreasonable to expect as little as a simple "thank you" for busting my tail day after day? Maybe, just the slightest recognition that I am here, working hard, doing the best I can?
Administrative assistant in a state agency

When we receive no recognition at all, Xers sometimes wonder if managers even know we are working there. These managers reinforce Xers' natural skepticism about the value of investing in institutions like employers and provide signals to Xers that we can expect little reward for working hard. Xers don't define ourselves by bonus pay, raises and promotions. But these things still count. Managers who refuse to give Xers credit where credit is due, encourage the rapid divestment of Xers' creative assets.

"I Want Some Recognition"

Did you ever have to tell someone how good you are just to get a little credit? Recently my team launched a new magazine from the point of conception to the newsstand. At the public launching, my manager was there, bowing...taking all the credit, down-playing our role. That really bothered me, because I worked my ass off on the project. This was the time for him to recognize my work publicly. If I work really hard for you, I want some recognition.

Associate general manager for development in a magazine company

XERS' AMBITION IS A QUEST FOR PERSONAL SECURITY

"A Little Pat On The Back"

No news is good news. Occasionally, one of the attending physicians, usually one of the younger ones, will give me a little pat on the back. But, that is the real exception. The lack of feedback can be demoralizing.

Physician in surgical residency

Recognition Needs To Come More Often Than A Blue Moon

He appreciates things, but you would really have to know the guy to know that he was appreciating you. The way he expresses it is... once in a blue moon. I do the best I can, but it's harder to do it so enthusiastically well. I do give 100 percent, but I don't give 110 percent. You know what I mean?

Paralegal

XERS CAN'T AFFORD TO WORK FOR MANAGERS WHO WITHHOLD CREDIT

"It Looked As If There Was No Reason For Me To Be There"

I had one manager who was really bad about giving me credit for my work. We would go to meetings together, where he would make a presentation. I would have researched the matter and done all the preparation for his presentation. Then, throughout his presentation, he

would say "I took a look at this," or "I researched this."
He never acknowledged my work at all. I would go to
these meetings with him but it looked as if there was no
reason for me to be there even. And that was a real
disincentive for me to do a good job. It made me want to
screw him up and see who got the credit for that.
Associate at an investment bank

The Foolish Manager Takes All The Credit

When I came back with answers for this manager, he
would present the results himself and just take all the
credit. That gets the junior level people to feel that they
are just the worker bees and this guy is getting all the
credit. I didn't want to work hard for somebody like that.
Associate at a management consulting firm

MANAGERS WHO STEAL CREDIT LOSE CREDIBILITY

When managers integrate Xers' work into their end-products and fail to give Xers credit, it feels to us that they are stealing our work. With no hope of long-term rewards, our work products are the vehicles through which we hope to make short-term contributions that will prove valuable as short-term investments of our creative talents. When we offer our creative end-results, we are testing the waters—checking to see if we are in an environment which values the sort of investment we have to offer.

Only in an investment-friendly environment can we begin to use our creative talents to achieve the kind of self-building that will add to our personal security.

When we make contributions and our managers hoard the limelight, Xers feel as if we have made a bank deposit and it was credited to someone else's account. It feels like the embezzlement of our creativity. We are not likely to make a deposit in the same account again, having discovered a particular manager to be an unworthy trustee of our creative assets.

Xers See Fair-Weather Presence

They take all the credit if the work goes right and none of the responsibility if it goes wrong. These managers would get mentioned at a company meeting—their work was recognized in a big way. That was demoralizing for the people below who were really doing all the work. We couldn't believe that senior management didn't know what was going on, who was really doing the work. That was a big motivation killer.

Analyst at a marketing research company

"I Should Be Getting Some Reward"

When my manager doesn't take a stand to get me a promotion or a raise I get very frustrated and angry. If I am doing far more than the norm, I should be getting some reward for that. Am I supposed to stop working so hard or just leave the company?

Senior account manager in an insurance agency

Be Careful Of The Apathy That Lingers

Let's say you put out your best effort and it gets sort of sh#t on. Well, what's the point of working equally hard or harder the next time?

Senior editor at a newsstand magazine

WHY XERS GROW ANXIOUS WITHOUT FEEDBACK

Managers don't need to give Xers promotions and raises every day in order to satisfy Xers' ambition. In order to provide the feeling of personal security Xers are seeking, managers need only provide Xers with regular status reports on our job performance.

How regular? If we could, Xers would monitor our status at work the way we monitor our bank accounts with automated tellers and our social lives with voice-mail. That means that managers can easily provide Xers with satisfying feedback, as briefly as one sentence, as long as the feedback is readily available, specific and accurate. Xers want to have the freedom to produce our own creative end-results at our own pace.

Once we deposit those results in our investment fund—we want to be able to monitor the value of our contribution at our own pace, as well. We want feedback which functions like a ticker tape on our investment. Was that a good investment? Is it going up or down? Should I invest elsewhere instead?

The Xers who speak in this section describe managers who are unwilling to provide that ticker-tape style feedback. In many cases, the managers described here are unwilling to provide Xers with any status reports at all. When managers offer Xers insufficient feedback on our contributions, we have no way to plan our future investment of creative energy. Is our contribution valued? Should we continue to contribute our energies with the same managers? Do we need to refine our contribution next time? Should it be bigger or smaller? How could it be better?

Without feedback, Xers cannot improve. What is more, we have no assurance that we are succeeding at work—that our investment is paying off. The result is that Xers lose confidence, grow anxious in our work and start spinning our wheels.

Xers Look For True Motivation In Our Managers

I don't feel that I am managed at all. My manager never

yells, never criticizes, but he never compliments either. Sometimes it makes me wonder how he really feels about me. Am I really doing so well or is he just not telling me when I'm not doing well?
Associate general manager of development for a major magazine company

REGULAR FEEDBACK IS THE MOST IMPORTANT SHORT-TERM REWARD MANAGERS CAN PROVIDE TO XERS

"Wondering If My Work Was Really Fine"

I was a clerk for a federal court judge. I got very little feedback from her even when I asked for it. So I was often left wondering if my work was really fine or not. There wasn't really any reassurance from her and it made me very nervous about whether I was performing at the level that she expected.
Clerk for a federal judge

Denying Information Causes Anxiety

Nobody ever lets me know how I am doing. I would leave this job tomorrow if I could because I don't feel stable here. I am not sure how my work is or if I am producing enough work fast enough or anything. I am afraid of getting fired—like my job is always in danger. I suffer from anxiety attacks at work, which of course blocks my work incredibly. I keep feeling that maybe I am just no good at this. If somebody told me I was doing a good job, if they even said, "just keep working hard, you're doing okay," I would be less likely to be thinking so much about leaving....A lot of times I felt like nobody even really knew what I was doing. I was living in a continual state of anxiety about my work product, always living in fear that I was not doing things right. I am sure I was wasting lots of time doing things that didn't need to

be done. It might have made me work harder, but it made me work harder on things I didn't need to be doing.
Associate at a mid-sized law firm

DON'T GIVE XERS FEEDBACK ONLY WHEN THINGS GO WRONG

The Xers who speak in this section describe managers who provide Xers with plenty of feedback, but that feedback is unbalanced and, therefore, inaccurate. Rather than giving Xers a fair gauge on our success, unmitigated negative feedback diminishes Xers' feelings of personal security to an unnecessary degree.

Summarizing The Feedback Problem

You get almost no positive feedback ever, but, you always hear about it when you screw up.
Physician in first year internship

Because problems, crises and mistakes often require immediate damage control, these situations command the attention of managers. When a manager is pulled away from her schedule to address an urgent situation, she often expresses her unhappiness to the employee at the bottom of it all. That's why Xers always hear about it when we screw up.

Xers can learn from negative feedback, as long as it is specific, timely and accurate. However, without positive feedback to balance our learning, negative feedback can be very demoralizing.

The problem is that too many managers fail to make time in less urgent circumstances to praise Xers when things go well. Managers who spotlight failure without making time to spotlight success are giving Xers distorted status reports and incomplete snap-shots of our success potential.

After awhile, Xers stop learning as well from the negative feedback because we resent the fact that none of our accomplishments are getting the same amount of attention as our failures. In the alternative, Xers develop slanted perceptions of our performance, which diminish our self-confidence.

Whether we feel unfairly evaluated by managers or we develop our own misperceptions of our work, unbalanced feedback is so discouraging that it often sends Xers looking for new jobs.

"No Feedback Unless I Screwed Up"

There was really no feedback unless I screwed up. My general anxiety was reinforced by the fact that sometimes a senior lawyer would come in and criticize something I did. The feedback I did get was always somebody calling me on a mistake so I felt like the dumbest lawyer on the face of the Earth.

Associate at a mid-sized law firm

WITH NOTHING BUT NEGATIVE FEEDBACK, XERS LOSE CONFIDENCE IN OUR ABILITIES

Establish A Sense Of Perspective

She put the emphasis on what was wrong versus what was right. Whereas of course most work is in the 90 percent range of being close and yet she doesn't focus on that. Of course, she has to point out what is wrong, but it feels like that's all she ever points out. It gets to me.

Marketing specialist for a heavy equipment manufacturer

Try Not To Say "It's Your Fault"

I was trying an experiment over and over again. My research director kept saying to me "You are screwing this up, you are not doing it right, it is your fault." I was so exasperated that I went to the library and found a paper which proved that what she had me trying to do was theoretically impossible. When I told her, she said "Don't come back to me until you finish it and I am giving you the weekend to finish." At that point, I sort of gave up and began looking into other research groups.

Research scientist at a major university

WITH REGULAR CONFIRMATION THAT OUR WORK IS NOT PAYING OFF, XERS START LOOKING FOR OTHER JOBS

"She Is Very Critical Of What People Say"

My department head says she believes that people should talk openly but she doesn't create a climate where people can do that. She is very critical of what people say, she will interrupt people and say, "I don't think that is very important," she rolls her eyes when people are talking. So a lot of people just don't say anything.

High school science teacher

Feedback Can Be A Distraction

My manager gives plenty of negative feedback but never a kind word. I feel like I am being treated like sh#t. He will leave me a message on my voice-mail criticizing something if he doesn't like it but I don't get a message when I do a good job. It's a distraction. I get sidetracked because I am mad.

Staff consultant at an information systems company

"Negative Feedback Hurts My Motivation"

Work is a top priority in our lives so positive feedback could be a very important element in terms of happiness at the office. I almost never get positive feedback, but I always hear about it if I f#ck up. When I am working my tail off, that kind of negative feedback really hurts my motivation.

Vice president at a major investment bank

WHY FORMAL REVIEWS ARE OFTEN NOT MUCH HELP

Most of the Xers whom I interviewed told me stories about formal reviews. Formal reviews range from annual to monthly. The formats vary considerably. Some reviews are written, some verbal, some have points and other measuring systems, boxes and charts and columns, some are based on specific categories while some are left open, some are based on multiple choice answers and some are based on freestyle essays. Some employers treat formal reviews as the basis for promotions and raises, while other employers don't value formal evaluations at all.

While Xers describe considerable variation in the frequency, format and weight which different employers give to formal review processes, most Xers report that the formal reviews by which they have been evaluated render inadequate gauges of their job performance—sometimes because they are overly positive or negative, but, usually because the evaluations are neither specific nor timely.

Most of the interviewees expressed serious doubt as to whether the formal reviews which they have experienced can provide the kind of timely, specific, and accurate feedback which Xers need to experience personal security in our jobs.

The Xers who speak in this section describe formal review processes which have been ineffective; which neither employers nor employees take seriously; reviews which focus on personalities instead of job performance; reviews which are unspecific, unprofessional, and unfair. One even talks about a review which drove an Xer to the brink of suicide.

An Anti-Climactic Bonus Check

Every year we get a formal review. But when they do that process they have hundreds of people dying to know what their bonus is going to be. The result is you get a three minute review, instead of really going over strengths and weaknesses. It is kind of anti-climactic. You sit there and listen and think "What is my bonus?" There are also supposed to be midyear reviews, which don't even happen at all.

Vice president at a major investment bank

XERS NEED FEEDBACK WHICH IS ACCURATE, SPECIFIC AND TIMELY

Going Through The Motions

A lot of the people go through the motions. The company has deadlines for when these annual forms have to be in. People dread it. Everybody knows they are due next Friday and half way through next Friday people are going to be sitting there making up objectives and evaluations.

Executive in a development program at a large chemical company

"It Was A Bunch Of Blanket Comments"

When I did have a formal review, it was done by two people for whom I had done no work. It was a bunch of blanket comments that I couldn't relate to any project or work that I had done. If I had had more regular feed-

back, like "This is what you are doing right, this is what
you are doing wrong," I could have adapted my behavior
accordingly.
Associate at a mid-sized law firm

"It Was Like A Fraternity Rush"

People would sit in a room like a fraternity rush, at a
round table, and basically everyone who was senior to
the person being talked about would be included in the
round table. Once they were talking about someone
senior to you or at the same level, you would be asked
to leave the room. The evaluations were supposed to be
anonymous. But, everything that was said in the round
table was said in front of a lot of people so that anything
that was said was not ultimately anonymous.
Associate at a large investment bank

Office Politics Are Easy To Spot

They told me that people at my level don't get a top
rating because we haven't been at the company long
enough. But, it was pretty clear that my review was not
based on my performance. Instead it was based on
office politics. That was totally unfair.
*Fraud control manager for a major telecommunications
company*

"The Most Ridiculous Set Of Measures"

There was an incentive system which they called merit
pay. But, it was based on the most ridiculous set of
measures: a bunch of numbers applied to very subjec-
tive criteria. Anybody who wants to tell you that you can
ascribe numbers to someone's performance and that by
doing that you take out bias and favoritism is full of crap.
Marketing coordinator for a book publisher

REVIEWS WHICH ARE INFREQUENT, UNTIMELY, VAGUE, AND INACCURATE SHOULD NOT BE THE BASIS FOR RAISES AND PROMOTIONS

"She Wanted To Commit Suicide"

The way they set up the system, some people are bound to fail. If you are ranked 100 out of 120 first year analysts, that can be devastating. On the night we found out our rankings, one friend of mine found out she wasn't in the top tier and she wanted to commit suicide. She was genuinely considering suicide, crying her eyes out the whole night. She had given her whole life to the company for a year. She felt so cheated. We had to sit up with her all night long to make sure that she wouldn't hurt herself. Why wasn't her hard work recognized? Well, let's say it isn't the pure meritocracy it claims to be.

Associate at a large investment bank

CHAPTER 4:

Xers' Ambition Is A Quest For Career Security

THE ISSUE OF XERS PAYING DUES

Perhaps the most uniform complaint managers express about Xers is that we don't want to pay our dues—that Xers don't want to spend time in low level positions with low level responsibilities just because we are the new kids on the block. Managers complain that Xers are eager for success but we are not willing to put in the time doing the grunt work in the trenches, which managers claim all of Xers' forerunners were expected to do before they would see the light of day in any corner office. Dues paying in this context is seen as a rite of initiation—a protocol of hierarchy in the workplace.

In this respect, managers seem to resent Xers' resistance to dues paying more on principal than for reasons of practical significance. But Xers' perspective on dues paying is precisely the opposite of this. Xers are willing to do grunt-work of practical significance which is necessary for the success of work related goals or necessary to produce valuable end-products. Xers are willing to put in long hard hours. Xers are willing to earn our way up the ladder.

What Xers are not willing to do is to pay dues which, in any sense, are based on protocols of hierarchy or rights of initiation. The reason is clear—the traditional rites in the workplace have been part of an initiation to a club called job security, a club which Xers are not invited to join. For that reason, Xers are not willing to embrace the bottom rung of the ladder as a matter of course, despite the fact that those of predecessor generations may have done so.

Credit + Opportunity = Cost Effective Investment In X

What you really want is a manager who can position her people in the organization to get them in front of the big guys at every possible opportunity and give you a serious chance for meteor like advancement....I work best when my manager makes me feel good about my work and when I am seeing a lot of payback. I don't mind working hard when I know a manager is putting me in the spotlight, letting the top guns see what I am doing.

Corporate staffer in a health care properties company

XERS HAVE GROWN UP ON SHAKY GROUND, WE UNDERSTAND EFFICIENCY

Xers have no reason to believe that hard work and commitment to one employer will win us any kind of long-term job security. Xers went to work as Wall Street was adjusting to the October 1987 Dow Jones mini-crash, as real estate values tumbled, as blue chips like GM and IBM, and everyone else, prepared to get leaner and meaner, cutting costs and laying off at all levels.

Just like everyone else in the 1990s, Xers know that most of the window dressing is gone and no job is safe anymore. We are treated as expendable labor. With no job security, Xers can't afford to make too many personal sacrifices for our employers. We have to invest in ourselves and find managers willing to invest in our careers.

Xers Can't Afford To Put All Of Our Eggs In One Basket

No one felt that they were necessarily going to be around for a long time. There are consequences in terms of what relationships you might build and it means you don't invest in a long-term career. That means you have less of a stake in the work.

Researcher at a major television network

Because there is no longer a club, no longer any promise of job security, the patrician concept of dues paying is not an appropriate way of understanding Xers' contributions in the workplace. Rather, managers should look at Xers' labor in the workplace as a form of investment.

While Xers may be reluctant to pay dues in the traditional sense, we are eager to invest. But, Xers are only willing to invest with managers who are attentive trustees to Xers' investment—managers must be willing to value Xers' contributions, provide the ticker-tape for ongoing appraisal, and pay some form of regular dividend.

SUCCESS WITHOUT TANGIBLE REWARD IS A WASTE OF XERS' TIME

There can be little doubt that Xers are fiercely ambitious. Moreover, the Xers who speak in this book are the most ambitious members of an ambitious generation—staying in the rat race against all odds and succeeding. Xers insist on short-term markings of success, regular indications that our investments of time and energy are not being wasted. What is more, our ambition is unyielding. But, for a generation which sat out the eighties waiting in vain for financial rewards which would never come, Xers' ambition is also surprisingly modest.

We are ambitious less for money and luxury than for safety in a dangerous world, for a new kind of life-long career security in a world where institutional employers do not offer life-long commitments. That kind of security can only reside in ourselves. This is why Xers need to collect constant evidence of our growing value in the form of short-term rewards.

Of course, to Xers, being criticized for wanting short-term rewards by managers who were the very yuppie-fast-buck-artists of the eighties who soaked the money river dry is an irony too vivid to ignore. It is particularly ironic, considering that Xers' desire for short-term indications of our success is largely driven by the lack of job security in today's working world, a condition which was greatly exacerbated by the same spendthrift depletion of resources which benefited the eighties' profiteers.

Xers are not fast-buck-artists. But we are also not in a position to make long-term investments with our hard work in an environment which promises no long-term rewards.

DON'T BE MISLED BY WHAT SOME PEOPLE MISTAKE FOR ARROGANCE

What many managers perceive in Xers as excessive ambition is really an effort to integrate our careers into our quest for secure ground in an insecure world. The fact is, with fewer and fewer jobs available and many talented people looking for work, Xers are forever confronted with the reality that we are easily replaceable to most employers—there is always someone (often another Xer) waiting to step in when an Xer leaves. No matter how talented any one of us might be, most Xers feel like disposable labor—the paper plates of the job market.

Feeling disposable has greater poignancy for Xers than the mere confirmation that there is no job security in our era. The feeling of disposability resonates deeply with both the images we carry in our heads documenting the decay of Planet Earth and with the instantaneous and disposable products we experience through commodity culture.

Fungibility and immediacy are powerful themes informing Xers' view of the past and future. Xers grew up with powerful images of economic, environmental and social decay—national debt, personal debt, homelessness, global warming, toxic waste, AIDS, violence, crime, depression, pollution, epidemic, victimization, extinction.

At the same time, the commodity culture of instant gratification has created in Xers the expectation of fast results—money from ATMs, microwave meals, drive-up windows, self-serve food, convenience stores, self-serve gas, remote control and viewer's choice television, weather from the Weather Channel, sports from the Sports Channel, news from the News Channel, and everything else from the everything else channels. Xers are used to getting short-term results in a world which seems to hold very little promise for the long-term.

"I Should Have A Quicker Return For My Hard Work"

The biggest disincentive for me is when the career ladder is too long. In my 90 day review, my manager went over raises and promotions, all of which seem slower and smaller and less chance for growth than I would like. I feel like I should have a quicker return for my hard work. It doesn't have to be a huge return, and it doesn't have to be money, necessarily. I just want to make sure that I

am not wasting my time here.
Analyst at a major credit card company

THE STAR X FACTOR · LEADERSHIP IN THE NEXT MILLENNIUM

Managers need to realize that Xers' impatience for rewards and success is not an indication that we don't want to work hard. As the Star Xers who speak in this book make clear, Xers are ready, willing, and able to work hard—maybe harder than anyone since the Depression-babies. What is more, we are prepared to work better, to maximize technology, to bring our creative energy to bear on problems, to find innovative solutions. Working better is our investment system—creative results are the most valuable assets we have to contribute.

Xers just want managers to punctuate our efforts with some regular confirmation that our hard work is paying-off—in growth and learning, recognition, opportunity, good will, status, or even money. If managers want Xers to invest our best work, they will realize that Xers' desire for short-term markings of success is an opportunity for managers to reap the fruits of short-term productivity. Given the right incentives, Xers' ambition is precisely what drives us to go that extra mile every day.

"I Guess I Am Jumping The Gun"

I am obviously a high achiever, but I am stepping on toes here. Whole legs, actually. I guess the problem is that I am trying to make substantive recommendations on proposals they were giving me to proofread. I guess I am jumping the gun—that isn't supposed to be my job yet. I am trying to exceed their expectations and in the process I am exceeding their exasperations. The thing is

that I am trying to impress them, to get to the point where I can be sure they are happy with what I am doing.
Staff assistant at a big six accounting firm

Xers Want The Responsibility And The Opportunity

I am working in a hospital out in the middle of nowhere because I know that this is going to lead to a much better position faster than any other route I could have taken. I chose the current position because I want the responsibility and the opportunity for advancement on the fastest track available.
Associate administrator of a small hospital

OPPORTUNITY IS A TANGIBLE REWARD BECAUSE THE FUTURE IS UNCERTAIN

What are the right incentives, if not dollars, with which to motivate Xers to invest our most creative efforts with our managers? The answer is easy—Xers want managers to participate in our self-building quest for career security. One way the managers described in this section are participating in Xers' quest is by providing regular confirmation of Xers' own creative talent and recognition of the value of our work products. What do Xers want, anyway, a medal? Yes, that is exactly what we want.

We want proof that we are making it, proof that our work is being appreciated, proof that we can show to someone else, somewhere else, when we are sent, inevitably, on our way in search of a new job. It is no good to Xers to have just one manager keeping to himself his admiration of our work. We want managers to share that admiration, to give us public recognition. Not just to feed our egos—although that is a pleasant collateral benefit of public recognition. We want that recognition because it means exposure to opportunity, which means greater potential for future security.

Increased potential is a valuable incentive in a climate of limitation.

Beyond this, the challenge for managers is how to hold on to Star Xers who need continual feedback, affirmation and a sense of value in an organization. The best answer: Delegate valuable end-results. Give us a chance to add real value in the process—rather than delegating just the chores.

These needs might make Xers sound demanding and even insecure. But we are not. Our background makes us efficient and—if we find the right place—deeply committed.

"Giving Them The Best They Have Ever Seen"

Why do I love it? Because it is very intense, very challenging. Because the work we are doing is very effective, it produces numbers. Plus, our clients expect a certain amount of pro-activity, a lot of added value thinking, constant thinking, and not just delivering the minimum in what they expect. But instead we are giving them the best thing they have ever seen. That feels great. The company, the environment is terrific, I feel psyched to be working here. I know when I am doing a good job and I know when my work is being valued.

Assistant account executive at a major advertising firm

HOW YOU CAN INVEST IN XERS' QUEST FOR CAREER SECURITY

Managers who are beginning to understand Generation X already know that Xers' intense ambition is part of our quest for security in this unstable world. Xers are ambitious for regular confirmation of our success at work because we are working on short-term contracts—we provide managers with valuable work products in exchange for managers' commitment to making us more valuable commodities in the workplace.

We will readily invest in our managers' success when our managers are willing to invest in our careers. Because our work-repertoires and creative abilities represent the only long-term assets on which we can depend, Xers' own sense of personal security is closely linked to the rewards and opportunities which only managers can offer.

Smart managers realize that they can win Xers' loyalty and earn our commitment to short-term productivity by investing in Xers as individuals.

Xers think of ourselves as the sole proprietors of our own creative prowess—we have to be entrepreneurial with our skills and abilities in order to build within ourselves portable assets for the future. Thus, entrepreneurial Xers are creating a new kind of career security which fits with the economy of the future—a career security which is not tied to any one company, manager, customer or client. Xers are building a form of career security which resides within ourselves.

One Good Experience Includes A Measured, Confident Approach

My manager is very effective at measuring people's performance. He talks with us regularly about how our work is going and it is very clear that before he sits down to speak with someone, he has thought it out very well. He is very balanced and very specific in what he says to people, so you know that he is honest, that he is trying to be helpful. His feedback is very credible.
Sales associate in an electronics company

THE MODEL: F-A-S-T...FEEDBACK WHICH IS ACCURATE, SPECIFIC, AND TIMELY

Xers have a new deal to offer managers. If you cannot offer us a lifelong commitment of job security, that is okay because we have a lifelong commitment to ourselves. Xers are prepared to market ourselves and our abilities over the course of a lifelong career, just as if our time and energy were commodities we sell in a retail store.

Like any proprietor, though, we cannot sell to the highest bidder in terms of cash only—not if the highest bidder is going to take our best stuff and leave the store a mess, be a one-time customer and not even tell her friends and colleagues, leave us with no inventory and no way to replenish.

If you want our best creative products, help Xers replenish our inventory—facilitate learning and growth and the development of new skills. Be a good customer and try to leave Xers in better shape than you found us, not battle weary and scarred and disheartened. For goodness sake, tell your friends and colleagues about us—we can't afford to have just one customer. Most of all, try to remember, we may be working for you now, but really we are in business for ourselves—so try to respect us as entrepreneurs of our skills and abilities. If you can't do that, we will have to find other customers.

The best managers invest in Xers' proprietorships by recognizing and helping us to improve the value of our skills and abilities, by marking our daily successes, by exposing us to senior managers, and creating opportunities for career building and leadership.

The Xers who speak in this chapter describe managers who provide powerful incentives for Xers by offering Xers the short-term rewards which lead to our personal security—regular constructive feedback, regular confirmation of our successes in the workplace and opportunities to succeed further. When Xers know that our hard work is paying off, we are more confident, more productive, and ready to invest our most creative efforts.

"Both Positive And Negative, But In Regular Doses"

I get both positive and negative feedback but I get it frequently in regular doses. I certainly appreciate the positive because so often managers only give you the negative. It is good to know when I am doing something well and it is nice to feel appreciated. If I feel better about my work I am going to enjoy it more and I am going to be more productive.

Staff assistant in a subcommittee of the United States Congress

Xers Learn Best When We Can Discuss Ideas

We sit facing each other and work together constantly. There is a lot of hands on informal feedback, like "that's a good idea," "I like the way that sounds," or "maybe it would sound better like this," or "the next time you handle something like this I would like it if you would try this other technique." I learn best when I can immediately discuss an idea or an approach that way and get immediate feedback. It gives me more faith in my manager to have insight into what aspects of my work I need to improve if we talk about it right away.

Junior account executive at a mid-sized PR firm

"He Is Specific...I Know Which Things I Am Doing Well"

This guy makes an effort to say "thank you," and it is kind of interesting to me that it actually makes a difference. It makes a huge difference to me, especially because he is very specific when he says "thank you," so you really know that he means it and also it helps that he is so specific because I know which things I am doing well. It just feels like I have his respect and appreciation. **Associate at a big law firm**

RESPECT AND APPRECIATION EARN RESPECT AND APPRECIATION

You may have noticed that the Xers who speak in this book, and particularly in this chapter, do not emphasize financial rewards as a prime motivator. In fact, of all the Xers whom I interviewed, only a handful of lawyers and investment bankers are being paid huge salaries for the work they do.

The figures, common knowledge to some, are shocking to others: top law firms are paying Xers annual salaries of seventy, eighty, ninety thousand dollars, and more. Investment banks are paying hundreds of thousands to Xers after only a few years of work. One of these high priced Xers said to me "When they are paying us that kind of money, they figure they don't have to manage us at all." While it is true that astronomical salaries are a powerful incentive for the long line of talented Xers waiting to bend over backward for these top paying jobs, in reality, the top paying jobs are increasingly far and few between.

It is the rare manager anymore who can afford to lure and keep young talent with dollars alone. In fact, most managers are trying to pay their young stars less and less—starting salaries and pay scales have remained stagnant and downsizing has left smaller teams doing more work.

Because managers who understand Xers know that the job market offers us no long-term security, they know that we are looking for short-term payoffs. Many have a hard time creating powerful incentives without paying astronomical salaries and huge cash bonuses. How can managers meet the challenge of building loyalty and commitment, even to short-term quality, among a population whose careers can never be about any one manager, any one company, any one customer or client?

"He Goes Out Of His Way To Recognize Small Successes"

I had an instant rapport with my manager and our relationship is seamless. There is an ongoing constant feedback loop between us, which gives me a real feeling of security. He goes out of his way to recognize small successes and he always takes an extra minute to add a personal note to the recognition.

Assistant to the VP of human resources for a chemical manufacturing company

WHAT IS A CONSTANT FEEDBACK LOOP?

Managers who want to encourage Xers' self-building process offer Xers feedback which facilitates learning and growth, regular feedback which is accurate, specific, and timely. Just as Xers grow anxious without any reliable status reports on our job performance, we grow more confident and secure when managers provide regular indications of our progress, and steady confirmation of our value.

The Xers who speak in this section describe managers who are building constant feedback loops around Xers' work by integrating brief feedback sessions into their daily interactions with the Xers whom they manage. These managers help Xers' maintain confidence and productivity by recognizing every result, celebrating every success, treating every mistake or failure and every achievement as an opportunity to learn, and making every word of feedback accurate, specific and timely.

"He Always Lets Me Know When I Am Doing A Good Job"

He will say to me, "That presentation wouldn't have gone nearly as well if it weren't for those slides you prepared." It feels really good. Here it's all trust. I have this feeling that my boss really wants me to learn and to succeed here, because he always lets me know when I am doing a good job.

Analyst in a small investment bank

"Getting Feedback The Next Day, We Knew When We Were On Target"

We would turn out a product and then we would be getting feedback the next day, often based on the reaction or the news on an issue. But, the feedback is always going to be pretty clear on what goes right and what goes wrong. We would even hear, through our manager, when the President of the organization was particularly happy with something. That also made it a lot easier to take the negative feedback when things didn't work out as well. At least, we knew when we were still on target because we were getting it right most of the time.

Research assistant in a public interest organization

Feedback Is The Manager's Most Effective Tool

The executive editor will call on the phone or peek her head in all the time and say "good job" or "that piece was horrible before you got to it...but it looks really great now." It seems like something she learned in a management class. But, it is good because at least I know when I am doing something right.

Associate editor of a newsstand magazine

Bombarded By Positive Feedback

When I came here, I was bombarded by positive feed-

back. That gave me more confidence and made me want to take on more challenges and do a better job than I was doing. The management style is a combination of always having the time for people and being consistent with people. We also talk about problems regularly, whether we are happy or not. With all the positive feedback, I have to produce results.
Account manager for an insurance company

Creating An Atmosphere That Celebrates Success

They do so much to recognize every little accomplishment, they even give out mugs for pretty minor successes. It's just an atmosphere where they really celebrate success. When someone gets promoted here, they send around a "blue memo" (they call them that because they are on blue paper). When that happens, people in the company send back a note on the blue paper, congratulating the person for being promoted. When I got promoted, I got notes from people I had never even talked to. And the chairman of the company sent me a note, a personal note. When I pass him in the hall, he says hello to me by name, and this is not a small company. That sort of constant pat on the back is a real incentive to keep producing.
Assistant account executive in a major advertising firm

HOW THE BEST MANAGERS ARE INVESTING IN XERS' CAREERS

The root of most every Xer's career ambition is a perceived need to pursue a long-term plan to market our skills and abilities in an unstable economy. Managers who understand this about Xers know that they can create powerful incentives for Xers simply by keeping us in the line of opportunity and success. Doing so involves a simple equation that should serve managers well: opportunity for Xers equals responsibility for end-results plus exposure.

This equation is the key to giving Xers the ownership of our work which is the most powerful motivator of all. Managers who follow this equation will find their investment in Xers' careers paying off quickly because Xers will always maximize real opportunities to showcase our creative talents.

Real opportunity is an invitation to go more than the extra mile—you will find Xers unwilling to turn away from the creative process, willing to put in the longest days, solving problems you didn't know about, creating solutions no one has thought of, fine tuning and polishing our end-results and thanking managers for the chance to work so hard.

INVESTING IN XERS' CAREERS EARNS A BIG RETURN IN CREATIVE ENERGY

The Xers who speak in this section tell stories about managers who give Xers real responsibility for end-results and go out of their way to spotlight Xers' work whenever possible. These managers are willing to give Xers the credit we deserve because they know that is the key to getting our greatest productivity and our most creative results.

Managers who make a genuine effort to expose Xers to more senior managers as well as important clients and customers know that they are motivating Xers to succeed by our own labor—they pose the challenge we are eager to face. These managers hit the jackpot by recognizing that they have it within their power to invest in Xers as sole proprietors of our talents and abilities and become our most valued customers.

Making Success A Self-Directed Goal

My goal is to move up and be successful. This manager is always willing to help me in achieving my own goals, he wants me to succeed. His goal is not just to have a successful operation but to have successful people be promoted out of his operation.

Sales associate in an electronics company

"They Are Giving Me Opportunities To Excel"

The people in the agency treat me as if they see a lot of potential in me and they have been very good about giving me opportunities to excel. I was promoted after my first ten months here and I feel great about the place. That is the reason why 100 percent of my creative energy goes into my job.

Assistant account executive at a major advertising firm

"My Manager Is Building My Credibility"

When we meet other people, my manager introduces me as her "colleague." That is just one way that my manager is building my credibility when we deal with other people.

Program assistant for a nonprofit foundation

EXPOSING XERS TO OPPORTUNITY - CAREER BUILDING
"My Manager Has Been Loyal To Me. He Knows He Can Count On Me"

My manager has been very loyal to me. He has supported me, he has tried to push me along here, in terms of getting raises and promotions. He is always giving me responsibilities that are pretty high profile, bringing me into meetings, and if I have done the work letting me do the talking, and he sits back, and he is not uncomfort-

able with that. Because of that, he totally relies on me, he knows he can count on me, and he knows I would always go out on a limb to make things work for him.
Associate general manager of development for a major magazine company

"He Wants Us To Succeed...We Want Him To Succeed"

My boss is very aware of what he can do for my career and he goes out of his way to help. As research associates, we get invited to dinners, staff meetings, board meetings, and it is partly because he knows that is a great opportunity for us. Just inviting me to a dinner is incredibly valuable, because I can't help but be seated next to really impressive people who can really help me in the long term. He is constantly looking out for things he can do to help us. We are included in all of his staff meetings, with all of the very senior people. What kind of loyalty do you think that breeds? We practically kill ourselves for him. He wants us to succeed so we want him to succeed.
Research associate for a nonprofit foundation

Look For Ways To Promote Your People

My manager is always looking for ways to put my work and what I have done before the most senior people to get me recognition. She is very conscious of getting me recognition for what I have done and she makes me feel like I have a big future in the company. How can I help but feel good about her?
Account executive in an advertising firm

XERS WILL GO OUT ON A LIMB FOR OUR INVESTORS

Are Xers ready to lead in the workplace of the future?

Ready or not, Xers will be the leaders of the next millennium. Xers worry about the future of the world which we are destined to inherit, but we are up to the challenge of leadership. The Star Xers featured in this book are future managers, CEOs and CFOs, Army generals and Navy admirals, local civic leaders, governors and members of congress and cabinet secretaries and presidents, doctors, lawyers, teachers, engineers, scientists, book and magazine publishers, playwrights and authors and movie tycoons and Nobel laureates—future leaders of commerce and industry, the military, politics, medicine, law, education, science, and culture.

STAR XERS ARE ALREADY FACING THE CHALLENGES OF LEADERSHIP

Many of the Xers whom I interviewed are already on the fast track to leadership, making important decisions every day, rising to positions of responsibility and authority at very young ages, leading teams and sometimes whole organizations to success after success after success. Those who have not yet risen to that level are eager for leadership opportunities.

The Xers who speak in this section have already faced the challenge of leadership and are ready for the responsibility that comes with it. Uniquely prepared for the workplace of the future, Xers are prepared to lead organizations into the next phase of the information revolution.

Managers who help Xers reach leadership roles are engaging in the most meaningful form of career building. They are preparing the way for the future success of their own organizations and, more important, helping to ensure that Planet Earth will be in good hands when Xers assume the helm.

"If I Am Closest To An Issue, I Should Make The Decisions"

Now that I have a team of my own, I can make decisions. If I am closest to an issue, to a decision that needs to be made, then I should have the authority to make the call. That only makes sense, because, in the reverse situation, my hands would be tied. Now that I am able to make decisions with my team about the issues we are facing together, that is the leadership factor.

Analyst at a major credit card company

"I Am A Future Leader Of The Company"

We all take the leadership development very seriously. At the beginning of every new project, we put together a development plan for how each of us can grow professionally and personally in the project. Who is capable of taking a leadership role? Who can motivate people? Who can execute and deliver results? The satisfaction is amazing, the rewards and the recognition, the fact that I am a future leader of the company absolutely accelerates my motivation and commitment.

Corporate auditor in a global industrial giant

Xers Want To Take On The Challenge Of Leading

I am already at a point in my career, even at this age, where I have a chance to redefine the effectiveness of an entire organization. I am presented with a tremendous leadership opportunity. The guy who runs this organization approached me about succeeding him here. That puts me in a unique position because it increases my burden of responsibility. It doesn't help if we all just pat each other on the back and go on wasting all of our time on internal dynamics and how everyone is feeling today. Our mission has got to be putting out a useful product that matters to the people we serve as an organization. I

am going to have to take on the challenge if I am going to lead this organization into its next phase of life.
Executive staff member at a non-profit foundation

CHAPTER 5:

Xers And Corporate Culture

WHAT IS THE SIGNIFICANCE OF CORPORATE CULTURE IN MANAGING GENERATION X?

Corporate culture is a term used, for lack of a better alternative, to denote the practices and patterns of human interaction shaping the social environment in a particular workplace. These factors are critically important to the challenge of managing Generation X because they are often determinative in Xers' initial and ongoing evaluation of the potential for forming worthwhile institutional relationships with given employers.

In this respect, the significance of corporate culture to Xers is closely related to our internalized skepticism about the promise held by most institutional relationships.

In order to appreciate the significance of Xers' skepticism, one must be very careful not to confuse it with the youthful anti-institution rebelliousness of Baby Boomers—Xers' skepticism is not born of naivete and immaturity, nor is it born of a temporary idealism, but rather of shrewdness and experience and rational prognosis. Xers have grown-up during an era marked by a substantial deterioration in the constancy of social, religious, political, and business institutions. We have never witnessed the fortitude which institutions once offered their would be constituents. With good reason, Xers start out with low expectations for what personal benefits are made available to us by various institutional relationships.

XERS' EXPECTATIONS HAVE BEEN SYSTEMATICALLY LOWERED

As we look to the future, Xers have minimal prospects of enjoying the same long-term institutional dividends as did prior generations—from global debt to global warming, from job security to social security, the evidence is clear. Xers will continue in the future to rely on little other than ourselves for our security. We are ready for that challenge. Help in preparing for and meeting that challenge is the greatest benefit institutions can offer Xers.

While Xers start out expecting to fend for ourselves in a world offering few reliable institutional bonds, we also know that it is wise to watch for needles in the haystack—certain institutional relationships can be valuable to us in a world determined by such a high level of instability. Xers will gladly welcome the support of institutions in our pursuit of personal security.

Indeed, because work often provides the most significant and coherent institutional relationships available to Xers, managers can offer Xers help in building the firm ground we seek in our careers by shaping supportive corporate cultures. Institutions which support Xers in building that firm ground are the ones most likely to win our loyalty.

BUT XERS' RESPONSES HAVE BEEN SYSTEMATICALLY SHARPENED

Xers have learned to step cautiously in the world—and we read our surroundings very carefully. The signals of a given corporate culture define the texture of the institution, the promise of the relationship, the firmness of the ground. Is the ground like quicksand? Or is the ground strong enough to support Xers? Is the institution one which provides a source of temporary firm ground for Xers upon which we can continue the self-building necessary to keep moving on in the world?

Within the elements of corporate culture, are the signals which Xers read in order to answer these questions, in order to measure the ground around us and ahead of us, to determine whether we are better off staying put or moving ahead. The Xers who speak in this chapter discuss many different elements of corporate culture, but every element has a common thread. Xers reject cultures which undervalue the individual and make self-building impossible and, conversely, embrace cultures which welcome and support Xers and provide the temporary firm ground necessary for learning and growing.

RULE OF X: XERS WILL NEVER INVEST OUR BEST WITH MANAGERS WHO REFUSE TO INVEST IN XERS

Managers are wrong to think that Xers expect the world in return for nothing. When Xers express a lack of commitment to our employers, when we seem contemptuous or disloyal toward our managers, when we start the slow walk on to a new job, it is not because we are naturally disloyal or because we just can't sit still. Rather, Xers are making reasoned judgments about the likely value of investing in particular institutional relationships.

We make these judgments quickly because we have too much at stake and not enough room for error to be wasting our creative talents in institutions which fail to appreciate our value and fail to encourage our self-building. When managers sustain corporate cultures which undervalue Xers, they are communicating the very warning signals for which skeptical Xers are looking. Corporate cultures which undermine Xers' potential for self-building have no credibility with Xers—they confirm our skepticism, validate our inhibition to invest, justify our withholding of commitment and send us in search of more promising institutional relationships.

SOME CORPORATE CULTURES MAKE XERS UNCOMFORTABLE

Considering the volatility of the job market and Xers' amazing adaptability to change, it should come as no surprise that Xers who feel rejected by a given corporate culture will have no problem moving on quickly. To Xers there is nothing sudden about such moves. We are not restless malcontents.

We know exactly what we are looking for—institutional relationships which provide promising, investment friendly environments—valuable teams which support the individual, recognize Xers' hard work, provide ground on which Xers can continue building our selves, on which our value has room to mature. Why would Xers waste valuable time in institutions which do not provide this kind of environment?

The Xers who speak in the first part of this chapter describe managers who create corporate cultures which undervalue Xers as people, undervalue Xers' work, and undermine the self-building process. Xers told me about managers who want loyal team players but offer no leadership, no investment, no organization, no focus, and no recognition of Xers' value as individuals. Xers told me about managers who are out of touch and offer no vision, managers who are trying so hard to make their organizations lean they cannot see the human resources they are squandering, managers who only seem to get in the way, managers who are treating Xers like machines and then cannot figure out why we break down, managers who can't handle the growing diversity of the workplace and throw away talent their companies cannot afford to lose.

The stories in this section are glimpses of the kinds of corporate cultures in which Xers can never thrive—cultures where Xers want to minimize our investment and escape. After all, we are prepared to move on, to adapt quickly to another situation, perform a rigorous but rapid evaluation, and then decide to leave, or stay, as long as the environment cultivates self-building. As long as it does, we will stay and grow. If it does not, there is always a chance that the next institution will embrace us. Or the next one, or the next one after that.

WHEN THERE IS NO MISSION, THERE IS NO TEAM: THE JOB IS JUST A JOB

If managers want Xers to be loyal team players, they have to play a role in creating a clear mission for the team. Because Xers are predisposed to work on our own, to pursue creative end-results in our own space and time, it takes a special team to win our commitment. When evaluating a team, Xers look first for a clear team mission because a team without a mission is unlikely to produce valuable end-results. We are not about to abdicate some portion of our creative autonomy to a team which is likely to squander our talent. In order to subordinate our own goals to the goals of a team, we have to be convinced that the team goals are coherent and well defined and likely to succeed.

What is more, Xers are not likely to take for granted that team goals will be well focused simply because they derive from an institutional source. Quite the opposite, when team goals are institutionally driven, there is an even higher threshold of proof which Xers demand. The bottom line is that when Xers do not get to participate in the setting of team goals, when team goals are announced and imposed on Xers, the goals had better be darned good. The team goals had better be an opportunity to grow and learn—an opportunity to contribute to a valuable end-product. Because, in that context, the team goals will be the only point of reference by which Xers can define the value of our work.

LEADERSHIP CAN'T BE ASSIGNED...IT MUST BE EARNED

Managers who insist on defining work agendas and setting work goals without providing the leadership necessary to support the agendas and goals leave Xers frustrated and disappointed. With no control over goal setting and no leadership from the goal setters, there is no vision of the end-results to which Xers' work is contributing. That combination is the worst of both worlds—our creative autonomy is diminished and we are wasting time in directionless teams.

"We Have No Team Because We Have No Coach"

We have no team spirit because we have no coach. There should be more of a vision from above. There is no unifying mission, no sense of purpose. It would be nice to have people feeling like they are contributing to a whole, to the magazine as a whole. We are not being led, so people either give up or they fight for themselves only. Under these conditions, the product will never rise above mediocre.

Senior editor at a newsstand magazine

Denying Xers Explanations Serves No Purpose

The real turning point was when I started feeling like I worked for the company instead of being part of the company. Management did a complete reorganization of everyone's work life without ever consulting us at all, without getting input, without explaining what was happening or why. We were not included in any way at all. It did a lot of harm to morale and everyone's productivity dropped quite a bit. For myself, I had been putting in a lot of effort, a lot of extra time and effort. My interest in doing a great job kind of dissipated because there was such a loss of control. It made me feel like the work wasn't really my problem anymore.

Engineer

WHEN DOES LEAN BECOME MALNOURISHED?

Some managers think that Xers are just greedy for our share of the limousines, three-hour shrimp cocktail lunches, thousand dollar bar tabs, first class flights, presidential suites and other expense-account extravagances which we saw portrayed on television in the eighties. This flies in the face of experience, though. The extravagant eighties are ancient history and the lean nineties will turn into an even leaner first decade of the twenty-first century.

Today, corporate boards keep scrutinizing eyes on expense accounts and still find plenty of fat that needs trimming. Unfortunately, in their zeal to cut back from the heavy spending which marked the eighties, too many companies have gone beyond lean management to the point of malnourishment.

Xers are not greedy for more perks, although stingy managers provoke an ironic cynicism among those of us who watched the spendthrift eighties with a mixture of jealousy, awe and disbelief. Many of the managers who tell us we expect too much are the same Baby Boomers who proclaimed their anti-materialist values throughout the sixties and seventies only to become the sell-out yuppies of the eighties.

Now that the financial resources of employers are more limited, our Boomer managers can no longer lavish themselves, much less Xers, with the kind of corporate perks they enjoyed so recently. Still, many are reluctant even to provide the basic care and feeding which contributes so much to Xers' feeling of personal security in the workplace.

PENNY WISE, POUND FOOLISH MANAGEMENT UNDERMINES THE TEAM

Xers understand that financial resources are more limited now than they seemed to be in the eighties. But, getting lean has to be about more than cost cutting. Managers have to be able to tell the difference between fat and muscle, between junk food and vitamins.

What message are managers sending when they become so stingy with the slightest accommodations—a cup of coffee, a holiday party, a few minutes in the morning, a chance to make a telephone call, to take care of a small personal matter, see a doctor, have lunch, enjoy the job, have a little fun? These managers are telling Xers that our presence and our work product are not valued enough to warrant even the most minor investments in our well-being and comfort. That message only earns managers the scorn of Xers who already feel our entire future has been cheated by the wasteful spending of the eighties.

Xers Are Often The Ones Staying Later Than Anyone Else

One time my manager was trying to tell me how really important it is to be there on time, describing it as "9

a.m. the paper is read, coffee is drunk, and you are ready to work." That bugged the sh#t out of me because I stay much later than anyone else at the place. Most people work from 9 a.m. to 6 p.m. and I am there regularly until at least 8 p.m. It is totally bullsh#t. If my manager asks me to get to work early for a specific reason, I will get there before anyone and as early as he needs. I regularly arrive before he does. If I arrive at 9:00 or 9:20 a.m. once a week or every once in awhile and want to sit for a minute and drink my coffee, he should (be able to) accept that.
Junior account executive at a mid-sized PR firm

A Terrible Metaphor For A Whole Company

You had to sign off on supplies. They charged for coffee, you paid your own phone bill. They were very cost cutting on everything and cheap. People were always complaining about money, that they were underpaid, that they were getting screwed. We had to pay for our own Christmas party. Collecting the $56 for the Christmas party was a real hassle. Everybody moaned and groaned and complained about the money. It was like a metaphor for the whole company. The edict of the company is that everybody is replaceable. They pay nothing for loyalty. They think that is a bullsh#t cost. They attract mediocrity, because they underpay people and treat them like sh#t. That meant that they were always hiring people who were down on their luck, usually people who were fired somewhere else for good reason.
Bond trader

A Manager So Stingy He Lost What He Had

My boss was meticulous about hour counting. I never felt I could leave at 6 p.m., even if I didn't have a lot of work to do. We had only a half hour for lunch. I didn't even feel I could schedule a doctor's appointment. It was a huge deal just to make a doctor's appointment. There were times when I might be on the phone, obviously a personal call, which happens, and my boss would come in and stand in the doorway and just look at me until I got off the phone, a waste of his time as much as anything. It wasn't the kind of thing where everyone was on the phone all of the time. He would do it just to make a point. The guy actually thought that the minute his back was turned, no work was being done.

He was so stingy. He only had a part-time receptionist who worked Tuesdays through Fridays, 10 a.m. to 4 p.m. The phones in this place were incredible, hundreds of calls. Now, when do you think all of the calls come? People make calls a lot between 4 and 6 p.m., not to mention on Mondays. We had no receptionist during these periods. There were hundreds of calls and it was tough getting the calls, just having to answer them all the time.

The effect on morale was terrible, because nobody could get any work done. How did this affect our work? There were times when he would be in his office with a client and one of us would sneak out to the convenience store to get drinks for everyone. It was ridiculous. And, of course, we all took every sick minute we could, every minute off that we could, we got out of there every day as soon as we could, because we hated it. We dreaded going to work every day. And there was terrible turnover, which made for really unsteady workloads for the rest of us.

*There got to be this absurd feeling in the office of the
ten of us against him. From the attorneys down to the
receptionist, we all hated him. He actually joked about it.
We all figured he had to go on vacation sometime. When
he did go away for a week, we all worked doubly hard
the week before. Then we planned a day where we could
sit around the office and do nothing just to spite him. We
sat around and laughed every time the phone rang. Then
we all went out to lunch, had pitchers of beer. On the
way back to the office, we bought even more beer, came
back to the office and drank all afternoon. People were
even doing handstands against the walls. One of us left a
heel mark on the wall. The whole rest of the time I
worked there, all of us would go by that mark on the wall
and snicker. It was like our silent mark of rebellion.*
Paralegal in a small law firm

WHAT ARE YOU DOING WITH SO MANY MANAGERS?

Too many managers think that when Xers complain
about intermediate managers it is because we are arrogant
and don't want to deal with anyone but the top managers. It is
true that Xers resent answering to managers whose only role
is to fill another sphere of authority in the corporate hierarchy. Xers object to dealing with intermediate managers, just
like we object to dealing with other obstacles to our creativity.

Corporate cultures which have too many layers of management put intermediate managers in the role of obstacle
instead of facilitator of creative productivity. Xers have our
own mission at work—to be innovative problem solvers and
creators of valuable end-results. Superfluous managers cause

inefficiency and hassle and interfere with Xers' ability to produce those results.

Xers told me about hierarchical work places with too many levels of management, where managers are piled on top of each other, end-running each other, contradicting each other, and getting in everyone's way. Xers are getting caught in the middle, answering in all directions, getting fought over, and trying to manage all of the managers in our lives. When too much of Xers' time is wasted on unnecessary rivalries and unproductive management relationships, Xers cannot work effectively.

What is more, Xers read the signals of corporate cultures cluttered with managers—we see cultures which support authority for the sake of authority, instead of supporting individual creativity. That is why Xers seek to avoid intermediate managers and corporate cultures cluttered with them.

A Manager Bossed Around By Everybody Else Can't Manage

We had three layers of managers. The top guy sat in his office and managed the middle guy. The middle guy sat in his office and then came out only on scary occasions. My own personal manager was the lowest of them and she would get bossed around by everybody.
Chemical technician in the development lab of a major food company

INTERMEDIATE MANAGERS MAKE XERS' WORK ENVIRONMENTS CHAOTIC

"I Created This Little Place For Myself"

Our boss was the sales wizard of the company (and) a major stockholder. The boss-wizard's forte was selling— the managing was left to his assistant. I was supposed to

be working for both of them. She was like his right arm, second in command. But she was (also) defensive, self-righteous, and bitchy. We had to work around her all the time. What made that hard was that she was supposed to be the buffer between his sales team and him. There were a lot of factions and everyone had to work out their own little place for themselves and their own little relationship with the sales wizard. I created this little place for myself so I could work more on my own terms.
Commissioned real estate tax shelter broker

Juggling Intermediaries—And Dropping Everything

My manager has assigned someone intermediate to deal with me directly, but she is so hands on that she is always dealing with me directly. A lot of it has to do with scheduling. The intermediate manager will make a decision to try to do something and then the manager will come in and overrule that. Then he will come into my office shaking his head. It is frustrating that I am caught in the middle and having to deal with the two of them.
Staff consultant at an information systems consulting company

XERS CAUGHT IN THE MIDDLE WANT TO ESCAPE
"I Moved To A Different Part Of The Company"

When I first started working here, my manager lavished a lot of attention, gave me a lot of responsibility, told me about the strategic areas she would like me to cover. For the first five months, I was doing well in her department. After about five months my manager brought in a vice president to be in between her and me. That was awkward. I had already established this relationship with my

*manager. After this new VP came in, my access and
contact with my manager was severely diminished. It
became very demoralizing. All of a sudden the VP was
going to meetings that I was formerly attending and I was
no longer included. I ended up moving to a different part
of the company.*

Rising executive at a cable television network

The Servant Of Two Masters Satisfies Neither

*The tension arises when my manager and her boss don't
communicate well about how we should be spending our
time or about what their needs are for the day. If both of
them have a lot for us to do on the same day, then our
immediate manager gets irritated and loses her temper.
It makes things in the office very difficult, trying to
please two different people who make significant demands on me and my time.*

Aide in a political office in Washington, D.C.

WHEN XERS HAVE TO MANAGE OUR MANAGERS, THERE IS NO ONE LEFT TO DO THE WORK

"I Had To Manage Her Ego In Addition To My Work"

*Sometimes it became messy because even though I was
reporting to the person directly above me, I was still
responsible to the person two levels above me. I had to
please the person immediately above me and please the
supervisor too. But the account executive doesn't want
to hear that the supervisor went around her and came
directly to me. So I would have to manage her ego in
addition to my work.*

Assistant account executive at an advertising agency

Bad Situations Become Tests Of Will

*Two different lawyers were fighting over me. Each of
them would take me aside and tell me that I work for
him and give me a whole bunch of work. I didn't know
which one to approach or how to approach them and I
was working too many hours and too many days. I was
very annoyed, not at all impressed with their lack of
maturity. I thought it was a very macho mentality. It went
beyond how much work there was to do and became a
question of who was going to win out. I was the casualty
with the way it was going. I was going to quit if the
problem couldn't be resolved. Of course, eventually,
because neither one of them would give in, the paralegal
supervisor had to hire another paralegal to keep me from
quitting.*
Paralegal

"Look, Instead Of Wasting All This Time...."

*There were three hardware and two software engineers,
all in our twenties. Our manager was searching for an
(intermediate manager) to do the week to week managerial coordination. We went to our manager and said,
"Look, instead of wasting all this time looking for an
(intermediate manager), why don't we try working as a
team?" The design team had figured out a plan whereby
we would divide among ourselves all of the functions
that the (intermediate manager) would normally do. That
way, we would be working as a very close team and we
would each have been very willing to pitch in and help
each other....That was our solution. We felt there was no
need for an (intermediate manager). We thought that our
approach to getting the work done was very impressive
and would have made the project go forward on sched-*

ule. The manager rejected it out of hand, and actually kind of chuckled. This didn't make the team feel good, especially feeling like we weren't being taken seriously. After that suggestion was made, it was another six or seven months before there was an (intermediate manager). During that time, there was no red flag raised and of course he didn't let us implement our system of self management. By the time they finally brought in that (intermediate manager), four out of eight engineers in the design team had left the company and the project was a year behind schedule. Too bad for the company that our manager didn't trust our plan and let us take responsibility for the project.
Engineer

CULTURES THAT TREAT XERS AS IF WE ARE INTERCHANGEABLE WITH ANY ABLE BODY

Managers who want Xers to make personal investments in institutional relationships with our employers, need to participate in Xers' self-building quest for security. That means cultivating Xers as individuals. Instead, many Xers told me they feel like they are being used at work like infantry bodies or machines.

Far from being valued as individuals, many Xers are treated as if we are expendable, interchangeable with any other able young body. Our managers are disregarding Xers' individuality by promoting corporate cultures which fail to consider Xers' personal needs and leave no room for originality or creativity in our work.

One reason managers are spending less time investing in Xers as individuals is that, in today's economy, employers have the luxury of a buyers' market—there are a lot more young able bodies than there are good jobs. So, maybe Xers shouldn't complain. But, if managers don't invest in Xers as people, we will complain and we will perform below capacity and we will go ahead and quit our jobs.

Many managers attest they cannot understand why, one minute, Xers are haunting their offices unshaved, circles under our eyes, looking craven, stressed out, beaten down, chasing deadlines, and then, the next minute, Xers are quitting our jobs. These are the same managers who can't figure out the fax machine. The fax machine can't talk. Xers can.

Mismanaged Xers Feel Like Excess Hardware

I felt very much like a machine. She wouldn't attend to anyone's personal needs until they started to break down.
Research scientist at a major university

"Our Peers Are Being Used As An Inhuman Resource"

I feel like a person out of that famous war image of a front line of soldiers, where they get mowed down, line by line, only to be replaced by the next line. I feel like I am an appendage to a machine. I work too many hours, I am not in control of how many hours I work, I hate the work that I am doing, and the people I work with are horrible. God if anybody hears me, I am going to be dead—I am talking to you from work (at 11 p.m. on a Thursday night). It's kind of like jail. I work with these bankers who are remnants from the 1980s. I really feel like our peers are being used as an inhuman resource. There is one girl who works here all the time: she is like a living crucifix, like the image of suffering.
Analyst at an investment bank

IF MANAGERS TREAT XERS AS AN EXPENDABLE RESOURCE, DON'T BE SURPRISED IF XERS TREAT WORK AS AN EXPENDABLE RELATIONSHIP

Everyone Is Expendable? At A Given Time, Maybe Not

The philosophy is to hire a bunch of bright kids and teach them all the same exact thing. They want to produce a uniform product: a consultant. And everything the consultant brings to their clients is uniform, it is all the same work. They have manuals on how to do everything. They don't encourage originality or creativity. They want to train everyone the same and have everything standardized so that they can plug anyone into a project. That means they can just solve problems by throwing people at them. The rule of thumb was you would lose 50 percent of the starting class each year; the top 25 percent and the bottom 25 percent, so what they would have left is the mediocrity. Of course, they incur a huge expense training, but I guess they have an unending supply of people.

Management systems consultant

"Don't You Dare Leave This Company"

The first thing out of this manager's mouth was "Don't you dare leave this company in the first two years because I will lose money on you." He told us that the company loses money on us for the first two years and we had to stay around for more than two years, so that he could start making money on us. It turned me off to him a great deal. There were two other people at the lunch table with me, who talked about it with me after. When the headhunters started to call, (we) had no loyalty to him.

Information systems consultant

Reducing Enthusiasm...Encouraging Contempt

When I was thinking about leaving the company, I went to discuss it with my manager and he said, "Look, I need you on this project and if you leave this company I will do everything in my power to hurt your career." Basically my attitude, after that, was I am going to get through this phase of the project, do my job, that is it, nothing extra, and then I will quit. I had no sense of loyalty to him because of the way he treated me. With him, I stayed until the first available breaking point. I didn't have that loyalty to stay longer and put in all those extra hours.

Analyst at a major credit card company

Too Much Machismo + No Chance To Celebrate - Bad Management

I was told, "Let me give you a little something to think about: You're smart, but everyone here is smart. And, there are lots of smart capable people out there who are not working here, who would love to be working here. Maybe you should keep that in mind." In other words, you don't matter and are interchangeable with anyone else waiting to take your place. For intelligent people with creative aspirations and abilities, there is no way you can celebrate yourself in a firm with that philosophy. Most of what young lawyers do in a law firm could be done by an army of high school students anyway.

Associate at a large law firm

WHY ARE SO MANY CORPORATE DIVERSITY PROGRAMS FAILING?

A lot of managers are frustrated that their corporate diversity programs seem to be failing. Most companies have been trying to recruit women and people of color since the seventies. The problem is that too many corporate diversity programs end right where they begin—at the recruiting stage.

As a generation, Xers bring to the white collar world a uniquely diverse work force—perhaps the most highly educated and talented force of women and people of color that any generation in history has had to offer. Having been educated together as a very diverse and integrated generation, Xers have very high expectations for diversity in the workplace.

We have come to expect social environments which offer a more diverse mix of people and promote a wide range of perspective—we have learned that diversity fosters creativity. For these reasons, outright racial and gender discrimination in the workplace is particularly intolerable to Xers, regardless of whether it is aimed at ourselves or our peers.

RECRUITING WOMEN AND MINORITIES DOESN'T MAKE A DIVERSE WORK FORCE

While most companies accept the notion of promoting diversity in the workplace, too many managers are complicit in work environments which are far from welcoming of women and people of color. I am sad to report that among the Xers whom I interviewed, many of the women and people of color reported experiencing discrimination at the hands of their managers. Xers talked about facing hostility, pressure and condescending treatment—about a lack of role models, unfair reviews, and disappearing promotions.

While no one can thrive under the weight of discrimination, Xers who experience discrimination in the workplace respond vigorously. Xers are not likely to ignore the challenge, although we may not take to the streets to march. Rather, Xers who suffer discrimination are likely to refocus our own creative energies and kill two birds with one stone—pursuing acute strategies for our own success which also address the problem of discrimination we may have experienced.

I'll introduce you to one Xer who faced discrimination at the hands of managers in the bank where she worked—now she is a civil rights lawyer suing banks for racial discrimination in mortgage lending.

"Welcome To The Neighborhood"

I dealt with a lot of hostility because I was a new person in the company and because I am black. It was just one big bowl of problems. I feel that upper management supported the attitude of the lower managers in treating me like an outsider. On one of my performance reviews, the manager actually wrote that I did not make an effort to bond with the other people at my level. It would be like if I were new in a neighborhood that wanted to keep me out and I was supposed to go around and knock on each door and say, "Hi, I am new in the neighborhood. Welcome to the neighborhood. If there is ever anything I need, should I just feel free to call you?" How am I supposed to work in a situation like that?
Fraud control manager for a major telecommunications company

A Fact Of Life: Working Harder To Accomplish The Same

I am African-American, so there are issues that some of my counterparts don't deal with in the workplace. It is always an underlying issue in the workplace. There is always the question of whether I am being treated a certain way because I am black. I feel an undue pressure to prove myself. I feel I have had to work that much harder to prove myself and to get promoted. I have had to go after tough assignments to get to where I am.
Finance manager in an international company

"What Do You Want To Be When You Grow Up?"

My manager was a real male chauvinist. In meetings he put me on the spot. He would say things like "What do you think, being the modern working woman in the room?" He would massage my back during meetings with other professionals, even outside people. He said to me one night at a party, "What do you want to be when you grow up?" I said "President" and he thought I meant president of the company. His response was, "You are just like my daughter, you think you can attain anything." Of course, I meant President of the United States. When I told them I was quitting, I found out how valuable I was to them because they offered me a lot if I would stay. Of course, by then it was too late.

Risk manager for a real estate investment bank

BUILDING DIVERSITY REQUIRES AN ONGOING WELCOMING PROCESS

"I Didn't See Anyone Who Looked Like Me Succeeding"

There weren't any role models there for me partly because I am a woman and there are no women in power here. I felt that it wasn't going to be the kind of place I was going to do my best work. I never felt that I could be incredibly successful there because I didn't see anyone who looked like me succeeding there.

Associate in a mid-sized law firm

No Women Promoted—A Bad Sign

I was recently up for promotion. My sales figures were higher than anyone else's and I had received very positive reviews. But, I wasn't promoted. Seventeen men were promoted and zero women. I never thought I would encounter that. I mean it's the 1990s. That makes me feel very discouraged and upset. I just wanted to say, "Screw you and I'm going to leave." But, I didn't want to have sour grapes. I was very nervous about bringing up this issue because I don't want them to think I am falling back on being a woman. I want to be promoted because I am competent and capable but I also want to be on the same playing field with the men in this company.

Sales associate in an electronics company

He Has A "Problem With Women"

After I was there for awhile, four or five of the women lawyers came into my office, independent of each other, and told me how unhappy they were about the division chief. The general idea was that he clicks better with the guys and so they move up. He doesn't click as well with the women, so they are held back and don't get the kind of advanced work they should be getting and which they need to be getting to prove themselves. That was discouraging to me because that meant that morale was obviously really low among the women. Things like that hurt the morale. When I got there I thought, wow, this is going to be a team, this is the public sector, and yet, I now think that I was a little bit idealistic about the whole thing. That is discouraging.

Assistant corporation counsel in the law department of a major city

MANAGERS NEED TO BUILD THE RIGHT CULTURE, OR ELSE...

"Now I Sue Banks For A Living"

As a black woman, I experienced discrimination in two out of the three lending areas in which I worked. It had an impact on the amount of responsibility I was given and it affected my reviews. When I asked about a negative review one manager gave me, I was told that my skills needed improvement. I was told to do an exercise and make a special presentation both to my manager and to a fellow trainee who was supposed to be my peer. No one else was asked to do something like this. It was a humiliating and infuriating experience.

The other African-Americans at the bank were facing similar problems. The bank was actively recruiting African-Americans but had a hard time retaining them. Among African-American people who came into the program when I was there, most people left immediately after the two year training program. As it turned out, I scored in the top 5 percent of the training class in the exam which we all had to take. And just after that, I won second prize in a writing contest for all the banks in our region. I realized they were all wrong and I said to myself, "To hell with you people."

The whole experience prompted my decision to go to law school and become a civil rights attorney. Now, I sue banks for a living—for racial discrimination in mortgage lending. I get to use my banking knowledge and, each day, I say to myself, "Thanks for the memories guys." It keeps me motivated.

Commercial lender turned lawyer

HOW SOME MANAGERS CREATE CORPORATE CULTURES WHICH OFFER XERS SELF-BUILDING AND PERSONAL SECURITY—AND WIN OUR LOYALTY

Just as Xers will reject corporate cultures which undervalue the individual, so Xers will embrace cultures which cultivate the individual and support self-building. One of the most powerful strategies managers can pursue to engage Xers' loyalty is to recognize our value as individuals enough to justify making some investment in Xers' personal comfort and well-being.

Managers can create needle-in-the-haystack cultures without huge expenses of time and money. It is a matter of emphasis. Xers are looking for corporate cultures where we are welcomed as individuals and allowed to make our mark within the organization, cultures where we can grow as individuals, cultivate our ability to fend for ourselves, and build on our self-based career security.

What steps are managers taking to create self-building corporate cultures in order to win Xers' loyalty and commitment? The Xers who speak in the rest of this chapter describe managers who are creating Xer-friendly cultures—cultures in which managers maintain credible authority by staying in touch with Xers' work, offering clear signals that the work we are doing is important.

Xers tell stories about managers who maintain open channels of communication and authority, by actively seeking Xers' input on matters ranging from work schedules to final product goals and including Xers in important decision making as well. The managers portrayed in the rest of this chapter are winning Xers' loyalty by demonstrating loyalty to us—by going to bat for Xers with senior management and clients and other shared constituencies. These managers are earning

Xers' personal commitments by making personal commitments to Xers as individuals.

BUILDING AUTHORITY BY LEARNING THE DETAILS OF XERS' WORK RESPONSIBILITIES

Skillful managers know how to engage with Xers' work and maintain authority without imposing on Xers' creative enterprise. These managers build credibility with Xers as potential teachers by ensuring that they understand Xers' work responsibilities well enough to manage us. By remaining well informed about Xers' jobs and always having something to offer, these managers stand in diametrical opposition to the superfluous intermediate manager. They are facilitators of creative productivity, valuable players in Xers' enterprise, and, therefore, Xers respect their authority.

Just as Xers disdain managers who stand in the way with nothing to offer but pointless institutional authority, Xers trust and admire managers who understand the details of our work—the short-cuts and pit-falls, the obstacles we are likely to face and the time and energy required to achieve particular results.

Different managers achieve this credibility in different ways. In many cases, managers have actually performed the very same or similar job tasks now performed by the Xers they are managing—these managers have the most direct knowledge possible about Xers' work and the highest potential for empathy. Without such direct knowledge, most managers need to develop alternative strategies for understanding the work experience of the Xers they are managing.

In the following section, you will read about managers going out of their way to build understanding and the credibility that comes with it. You will read about one manager who temporarily demoted herself to perform a lower level job, just so she could walk in Xers' shoes for a while. Other managers are forming teams where managers and Xers work together to resolve issues which result from a lack of information flowing upward. Still other managers succeed with the most obvious strategy for understanding Xers' work experience: they regularly ask Xers how everything is going, they listen to the answers, and they use what they learn to become better managers.

"They Have Been Through It Themselves"

All of the managers in our organization have been out in the field, doing exactly what I am doing now. Because they have been through what I am experiencing, they know how to deal with it—both emotionally and on an operations level. They very often have some operating knowledge where I might be having a problem. Also, most of the managers have probably had more than one personal crisis when they were on the road. They know what we are going through, because they have been through it themselves. That makes it easier to work with them.

Corporate auditor in a global industrial giant

Know What It's Like On The Front Line

One time, the chief financial officer of our agency came to me to ask about a particular account. When I talked with her about it, she felt totally in the dark about all of the daily concerns I was raising. She told us to take one of our projects and put her on it start to finish because she wanted to learn what it was like to work in our department. She then had a much better understanding of things. She came out of that having a lot of respect for us and we had a lot of respect for her and wished that

*more people would do what she did. She has been much
more sympathetic to us since then.*
Traffic coordinator in an advertising firm

Focus Efforts On Fixing Acute Problems

*Now, we have teams designed to fix acute problems in
the workplace and the teams include people at all levels
of the company from me up to executives. The company
is trying to get everybody on all levels to play a role. The
idea is that by working together to fix acute problems,
managers will benefit from more candid interactions with
the people they are managing. It has really improved our
communication and effectiveness as a team.*
Associate at an investment bank

"Work Was Getting Done And Was Evenly Divided"

*Management knew if one group had too many projects.
They walked around and asked people what they were
working on and that meant that the work got done and it
was evenly divided. If one person was working consistently until 11 p.m., they saw the time sheet. The right
people knew that you were working that late. They would
realize maybe that you needed a hand on your projects
and that you were being overworked.*
Analyst at a marketing research company

XERS KNOW THE DIFFERENCE BETWEEN MANAGERS WHO PAY LIP SERVICE AND MANAGERS WHO VALUE INPUT

Managers who go out of their way to seek Xers' input on
important matters and include Xers in decision-making are
giving Xers clear signals that our contributions at work are

valued by management. They are also giving Xers the chance to improve our abilities by meeting challenging responsibilities. Just as Xers are reluctant to invest with managers who undervalue our work, we are eager to invest our best efforts with managers who place a high value on our efforts and allow our best work to benefit both our managers and ourselves.

Smart managers understand that they need to actively demonstrate to Xers that our work is valued by providing opportunities for Xers to make meaningful contributions. When managers seek Xers' ideas, opinions, and work product, when managers include Xers in decisions ranging from office moves to new employees to customer service, Xers know we are important players on the team.

With some creative input, Xers are more likely to feel a shared ownership in management driven decisions and goals, more likely to go out of our way to support and implement them, and to seek to find in them opportunities to learn and grow and improve our abilities. The results are a benefit shared by everyone concerned.

Pay More Than Lip Service

Even though the two other people on my team have doctorates in the area and I don't, my manager still considers my ideas. She respects my creativity and she doesn't just pay lip service. When she implements my suggestions, that really encourages me to be creative and present ideas.

Education policy aide in the office of a state Governor

Listen To Input From Everyone On Everything

My boss always asks for input from everyone on everything. For example, we are making an office move right now. And, he is so concerned about all of our commutes and how it is going to affect us. Another example, when we hired an office manager, he asked each of us for input and afterward, he asked each of us how we thought she was working out. He always wants to know what we think. Of course that makes me feel more like I am an important part of the team.

Analyst at a small investment bank

"It Encourages Me To Put In The Time And Really Try"

He really listens to his employees. He doesn't always agree, but if he disagrees it is never because he is discounting what I have said. Because of that, he gets a better product. There is a book we are about to send to the publishers. They have been working on it for two years. Because he asks for input and really wants input, our manager actually gets the benefit of our work on the project. I feel like I have edited as much of his work as he mine, and he not only accepts that, he wants that, he encourages it. It encourages me to put in the time and to really try to make the best possible suggestions, because I know he is going to take them seriously.

Research associate for a non-profit foundation

Make Xers Believe Our Work Counts

If my boss is working on a written product, he will give it to me to see if I have any input. I will make a comment or addition. He very often includes my comment. Of course, that means whenever he gives me something to read, I look at it very closely and give it a lot of thought, because I know he is counting on me. I know that my work might end up in a finished product. It matters because I am able to contribute more.

Staff assistant in a subcommittee of the United States Congress

RULE OF X: XERS WORK HARDEST FOR MANAGERS WHO IMPLEMENT XERS' IDEAS AND INCLUDE OUR WORK IN FINAL PRODUCTS

"No One Feels They Get Left Out"

The executive director is always trying to make sure that other people are included in making decisions. Even if it is a decision that he is going to make, he includes the people that should be there. Like with a budget, everyone knows full well that he was going to decide what the budget was and that he had his own financial considerations which might end up making the decision. But, he would still include the people who were involved with the decision. No one feels they get left out.

Admissions director for a non-profit educational organization

"She Always Asked For My Opinion"

My relationship with my last manager was fantastic. She was incredibly organized and productive. She always asked my opinion, wanted my suggestions. She was always soliciting my comments and advice. I felt really connected to my work and I really wanted to shine for her.

Real estate investment analyst at a life insurance company

Treat Xers Like Valued Sources Of Skill And Knowledge

My expertise is in an area which my manager doesn't know much about. I also know things about the market that he doesn't know, because we have different experience. He looks to me as a knowledge base. My skills and my knowledge are more appreciated.

Marketing manager for a major financial services firm

Don't Hesitate To Admit Weaknesses And Share Strengths

The first day I was here, my manager said to me, "You need to know, this is our program, not my program, and you and I are working together on this." She set out at the beginning the expectation that we would work as a team, which made a whole lot of difference to me. She includes me in meetings with all kinds of people and she even says that the fact that I start with less information and that I have less experience can be an advantage to her. She says my perspective contributes to our working together. When we go to meetings and conferences, we have a chance to get very different types of information because of our different positions and people's impressions and assumptions about each of us. For example, I will talk to the high level people who are a little more reserved with my manager and much less cautious when talking to me. My manager continually says to me, "I am so glad you are here with me because I wouldn't ever be able to get the side of the story you are getting." She is constantly pointing out that we both have strengths to offer, complimentary strengths. And that is what makes us a team.

Program assistant for a nonprofit foundation

Earn Xers' Respect By Going To Bat For Us

When I have a commanding officer who is going to bat for me, looking out for me, even if he is being a hard ass, I will go the extra mile.

Officer in the U.S. Armed Forces

HOW DO MANAGERS MOTIVATE XERS TO GO THE EXTRA MILE?

Most Xers have to operate in our jobs, at least at first, without much power of our own. This is not only because we are young, but also because Xers' relative transience in today's job market means we are often even newer to a particular employer than to the job market, per se. Having a lot of responsibility and no power with which to fulfill that responsibility can be a deeply frustrating experience.

When Xers need to approach someone in the workplace to leverage power on our behalf, we often look to our managers for support. It is usually the case that our managers are the only people whom Xers can approach who are also in a position to leverage power on our behalf. Managers who are willing to leverage that power by going to bat for Xers with senior management, customers, clients, suppliers, and other organizational constituents make it easier for Xers to feel comfortable and powerful in our work. That means Xers are able to feel safe going to bat for managers in sticky situations because we know we will be supported and not abandoned if push comes to shove.

It also means Xers will go out on a limb to achieve creative results. Like all creative entrepreneurs, Xers find our greatest achievements in the room we have to make mistakes. Xers thrive in supportive work environments conducive to achievement and creative growth. Managers who demonstrate their loyalty and commitment to Xers by creating such environments earn Xers' deep loyalty and greatest creative efforts.

"My Manager Really Backs Me Up"

When my manager backs me up, it reassures me that I don't just work for her, but that we are on the same team. It means I am going to stick my neck out, take chances, do whatever is necessary to get the job done.

Education policy aide to a state Governor

XERS WILL GO THE EXTRA MILE FOR MANAGERS WHO HAVE THE GUTS TO STAND BEHIND US

The Managers Took A Lot Of Heat Over Our Unconventional Styles

Our team didn't wear suits. We had our own style. We even wore ripped jeans, came in late, took long lunches. But our work was fantastic. We were the best scientists in the company. Our manager took a lot of heat over our unconventional styles. He was willing to compromise for the personal experience of the scientists because the quality of our work was so good. And everybody there was totally committed to doing a great job, totally into their work, doing more than anyone else in the company.

Research scientist at an electronics company

WHY A LITTLE CARE AND FEEDING IS SUCH A POWERFUL SIGNAL TO XERS

For Xers—raised in a society which atomizes the individual without supporting her, endangers the individual while offering few safe havens, proliferates a discourse of personal responsibility without parallel mechanisms for self-building—institutions which recognize and address our personal comfort needs appear like oases in a desert.

Just as Xers are provoked to criticize managers who force austerity programs on Xers because they are still paying the bill for the extravagant perks of the eighties, Xers have a special appreciation for managers who are still willing to spoil us a little bit—even in the lean and mean nineties.

Xers know that resources are tight and we don't want or expect a lot of corporate fat. But, as any dietitian will tell you, everybody needs a small layer of fat—a little fat provides insulation, allows the body to absorb critical nutrients, and prevents the body from burning efficient muscle tissue under strain. Offering Xers a little corporate fat is a gesture which has a minimal cost and pays disproportionate dividends in Xers' job satisfaction.

Smart managers are leading cheers at daily pep-rallies, ordering pizza and cookies, running health clubs and art galleries, giving Xers "fun budgets," hosting Lettermanesque Top Ten List parties, and patting Xers on the back. When managers invest time, energy and money in Xers' comfort, health and well-being, they are demonstrating a willingness to invest in Xers' personal needs. Xers, cautious investors that we are, are more likely to make substantial personal investments with managers who demonstrate a willingness to invest in Xers' personal needs.

"Wow, This Is Kind Of Weird"

Every morning we start the day with a company meeting. There are about 50 of us and the meeting starts off with a cheer, "Good Morning Everyone." Everyone sits in a circle in chairs and somebody says "How is everybody doing this morning?" Then everybody yells "Fantastic!" Then we do warm-up exercises. After that we have announcements and then two or three people will discuss the past week's performances and the next week's goals. We talk about our daily goals and our goals for the week. Every meeting is ended with a different cheer— somebody is chosen to lead an ending cheer and they get to make one up. The first few times I went to these meetings I thought, "Wow, this is kind of weird." But, these meetings are always really, really good. Every single meeting starts and ends on a really loud positive note and you get into the day and everybody's attitude is flying high. You get to have this great meeting, joke and laugh, cheer and get pumped up. It really gets your blood flowing.

Sales associate in an electronics company

WHEN WORK IS AN OPPORTUNITY FOR XERS TO FEEL HEALTHY AND HAPPY, XERS WORK LONGER, HARDER HOURS AND PRODUCE BETTER RESULTS

Simple Things Like Pizza Can Have a Big Effect

We had to work a lot of weekends in a row, which meant there was virtually no time off for several weeks. My manager was very cool about it. He didn't demand that we come in, but he asked us. When we were in on the weekends, he would order pizza, so there would be pizza around and at least it felt more like a special day. That was a little thing but it made a big difference in how it felt to have to put in all that extra time.

Researcher for an investment services company

Corporate Cookies May Also Do The Trick

On Thursday afternoons, they did something called "corporate cookies" and everyone would get together in someone's office and eat cookies. They had cookies delivered. That was the corporate department's policy to

build up camaraderie. The funny thing is that everyone looked forward to Thursday afternoons. Just for that one hour it felt like there was more to the job than just work.
Paralegal

The Wonders Of A Fitness Center

Every day I get a notice about a trip where the company charters a bus and goes on a skiing trip or to the theater. Also, they have a fitness center and they promote wellness. I go over to the fitness center during the day and it is packed with people working out or playing volleyball or running on the track. Of course, that kind of thing promotes happiness and loyalty to the company.
Executive development program associate at a large chemical company

COOKIES + PIZZA + EXERCISE - AN INVESTMENT IN XERS' PRODUCTIVITY

"I Could Focus My Energy On Something Else For A Little While"

The company has a health center with a full gym and a whole schedule of activities like aerobics, weight training, meditation, tai chi. We were allowed an hour out of each workday to go exercise. If I needed more time, that was okay. They thought that a healthy mind and body would inspire our work. It did. Not only was it a good break but it made the job very upbeat. Sometimes when you feel you are in a rut, or whatever, it is hard to get out. But here there was this whole other company sponsored activity. There I could focus my energy on something else for a little while and meet other people in the company. Being in an aerobics class, or whatever, with other people from the company, I got to see what other things were going on in other parts of the company. Not

165

to mention, when you have seen the VP struggling to lift weights, all of a sudden he is a little less intimidating than he used to be and that makes it easier to work for him. That kind of thing helps the company by fostering an attitude which breeds new and better ideas, a willingness to try new things, risk-taking, open communication, community. The company did not believe in sick days, at least they didn't call them sick days. I had vacation time and personal time, but no sick time. They don't believe in sick people, just healthy people with personal needs. They actually had an in-house art gallery where I could choose any of the artwork that I wanted in my office. That made me feel great about my surroundings, where I work. It made me feel like it was my surroundings, it made me more comfortable, immediately more at home, and gave me more ownership in the space and in the job. It made me feel like part of the company.

Marketing manager at a publishing company

XERS SPEND MORE TIME WORKING WHEN OUR JOBS ARE FUN

"Every Team Gets A Fun-Budget"

At this firm, 25 percent of a manager's bonus was tied to case team happiness, which was measured internally by an outside firm. There is also a big emphasis on fun. Every month every team gets a fun budget, which the project team gets to decide together how to use. Usually the junior people decide what to do with the fun budget, plan something, and then do it. This company is a much more profitable company and people are much more happy and productive than other investment banks where I have worked.

Associate at an investment bank

WITHOUT DAVID LETTERMAN, XERS' WORLD WOULD COME TO AN END

Top Ten Lists Remain An Xer Staple

Our organization subscribes to an information newsletter, which happens to print David Letterman's daily Top Ten List. During the summer when David Letterman was between NBC and CBS and off the air, the newsletter was having an ongoing contest where they were printing submissions of mock Top Ten Lists. I was brainstorming for ideas of a list on one of our issues that we could submit from our organization. I came up with one, but then we were told we couldn't send it out on the organization's letterhead. I was disappointed. But, then they let me organize our own inter-office Top Ten List. We had lots of submissions and had an office party on Friday afternoons that summer and gave out prizes for some of the best lists. It was fun and encouraged people to think about the funny side of our issues. And, I felt good that they didn't just shut me down.
Research assistant in a public interest organization

JUST ENOUGH FAT TO LEAVE A SWEET TASTE IN OUR MOUTHS

"Sometimes We All Go Out For A Nice Lunch"

Sometimes we will just put the phone on the answering machine and all go out to a nice lunch. Nobody gets left behind. Everyone goes. Granted, it is a small office. But, in a big company, you can do things like that with a department or a unit. You don't have to do it often enough to disrupt anything, just enough to make a difference. The other people in the office pick up on the mood. He is so generous that we are all generous to each other. And we are all generous with the company. I almost don't like to ask for time off, because I know he'll give it to me, no matter how much time I ask for or what I need it for.

Analyst in a small investment bank

Done Right, Even Kissing Can Motivate

The Chairman of the Board was always going around the company patting everyone on the back and kissing everybody. It was a kissing company. At least once a week the managers would come around kissing everybody and patting them on the back. It was an attractive, cool, smart, cutting edge company. The Chairman knew everybody. You pledged allegiance to the company and everybody made a lot of money. The people worked hard and there was very little turnover in the rest of the company. It was more likely that people would get married in the company than leave it. The people worked harder, they got better people, there were always good things going on and everybody knew everybody. I still am friendly with them.

Commissioned real estate tax shelter broker

WHAT DOES IT TAKE TO WIN XERS' COMMITMENT?

Smart managers understand that Xers' fierce individualism does not make us poor team players—but it does have an impact on our style of team participation. When management experts talk about "team management," a lot of them are referring to the Japanese model in which employees receive lifetime job security in exchange for their commitment and loyalty to the company team, which serves also as an axis for social life. But, job security is gone in America and Xers are not made for the Japanese style team anyway.

As skeptical as most Westerners are about the idea of subordinating their individual interests to the interests of a team, Xers wouldn't even know how to do so. Still Xers are capable of enthusiastic team spirit—Xers find sustenance and inspiration in shared experience, and we often find our greatest achievements are possible in supportive team environments.

"Being Part Of This Difficult Experience Together"

There is this thing about a bunch of people going through hell together. There is no non-doctor who understands what it is like to be a resident. There is a camaraderie. I felt a lot of personal support just from being part of this trial by fire that everyone else is sharing. And each of us becomes a doctor in his own right as we go through this experience together.
Physician in surgical residency

XERS FEEL SPIRITED ABOUT TEAMS WHICH NURTURE THE INDIVIDUAL

Work teams can be fantastic opportunities for Xers' growth, learning and accomplishment. Given the right elements of support and shared purpose, and given opportunities for each individual to influence outcomes and produce creative end-results, work teams can provide Xers with sources of temporary firm ground that are all too rare for us.

While Xers are most committed to teams which support individual accomplishment, the confluence of our individual commitments results in a deeper team spirit. Teams in which everyone is supporting each other by achieving as individuals are like firm-ground havens for Xer self-building. Such teams become almost like surrogate families for Xers, offering unique hybrids of emotional-creative support, which contribute further to our individual growth. We will express our commitment to the team by trying ever harder to improve and expand our own individual contributions and we will be glad to do so in pursuit of shared team goals.

Good Management Has A Personal Element

It is a very unusual law office because most of the attorneys are women and most of the attorneys are of color, so it is kind of like turning the traditional law office on its head. It feels very family like. We are a collective body where each person's concerns are felt by and supported by everybody. That makes it a wonderful place to work because it is more human, everyone feels supported here and able to be themselves.

Lawyer for a small public interest firm

"We Develop An Incredible Bond As A Team"

It is sort of like AA. We are all experiencing the same thing and we all lean on each other. Everyone in this job has wanted to quit many times because there are long days, difficult challenges. But, as a team, we help each other through those difficult times and help each other stay in this program. We develop an incredible bond and become a real support network for each other, which is good, because we are also a source of stress for each other. I rely on all of these people to leverage their experience, to give advice and help, because these are people of all nationalities and all backgrounds, and tapping into their knowledge helps me do better work. Also, I can always find someone that I can lean on, vent my frustrations and share whatever personal problem I might be having, which helps a lot.

Corporate auditor in a global industrial giant

Spread The Burdens And The Benefits

We have a team approach and a very high quality ori-ented atmosphere. We have scheduling meetings, so that everyone knows what everyone else is doing and we all help each other on all levels. Everyone's goal is to get the project done. I feel very supported in this team, like I can do the job I need to do and make a contribution that is going to matter in the end.

Analyst at a marketing research company

COMMON MISSION + STAR XER + STAR XER + STAR XER = X-TEAM-SPIRIT

"He Wants To Have An Aggressive Team Of Stars"

Our manager thinks if he makes us look good, it makes him look good. I have been in meetings with him and his whole game was not about who he was but about who we all are. Our manager thinks playing us up is the way to succeed. He wants to have a team of really aggressive stars. I happen to have a very cool boss.

Business development manager at a cable television network

CHAPTER 6:

Communicating With Children Of The Information Revolution

XERS' FACILITY CREATES MANAGEMENT CHALLENGES

What characterizes Xers, perhaps more than any other trait, is our great facility with information. It is true that Xers have a style of learning and communication which is unfamiliar to managers of older generations. To older managers, Xers seem impatient for answers, always demanding information, asking questions, and pursuing multiple lines of inquiry simultaneously.

What looks to some managers like a lack of attention in Xers is, rather, a rapid-fire style of interacting with information which comes naturally to us as the children of the information revolution.

Xers relate differently to information than our elders do because we were nurtured on the mechanisms and flow of the information age. Remember that Xers were the latchkey kids who baby-sat ourselves after school with computer games, television and microwave dinners. The greatest continuity in our childhood was a continuous stream of multivalent signals from multiple information sources—television, radio, telephone, computer-driven libraries, bulletin boards and indexes, voice-mail, faxes, and video games.

Xers have grown up accepting as our most available and reliable problem-solving resource the free-flowing messages of the information age.

The arrival of X is good news for forward-thinking companies because Xers are uniquely well suited to lead managers into the workplace of the future. We never had to integrate information technology into our work habits, so Xers do not experience discomfort with post-modern accoutrements. What is more, our high comfort-level and skill with the computer keyboard and CD-ROM, new software, new hardware, fax machines, voice-mail, E-Mail, on-line research, and the Internet are just the beginning of Xers' value in the workplace.

It is not just changing technology which characterizes the workplace of the future, but a changing atmosphere. Xers already know how to work in the virtual office where the only thing to grasp onto is your log-on password. We're comfortable in the virtual laboratory where inventors manipulate the elements of cyberspace. We're self-sufficient in the virtual marketplace where meaning is the primary commodity.

In every sphere, Xers' ability to cope quickly and efficiently with massive quantities of information in diverse forms is sure to be the key to survival in the twenty-first century.

XERS ARE USED TO HAVING INFORMATION AT OUR FINGERTIPS

Xers need managers who can keep pace with our voracious appetites for information—keeping open lines of communication and constantly refueling the work environment with challenging experience, new projects demanding fresh skills, and steady supplies of information, interpretation, and meaning.

When you're thinking about what Xers want, remember the electrical engineer who told me, "I want to be working in an environment where I face a new challenge every day, where I am learning constantly, where I have the opportunity to wrestle with the hottest new developments and expand my repertoire of skills so that I am always keeping up with technology." And remember the young woman working in human resources at a large chemical company, who insists that learning is her only condition for job satisfaction. "I am willing to work on anything in order to learn...I want to be working in an environment where I can constantly learn and expand my abilities," she said.

There is no way to alienate and demoralize Xers more quickly than to limit our access to information. Conversely, managers who feed Xers with great access to information and allow Xers the freedom to process information at our own rapid pace win Xers' loyalty by supporting positive learning environments and facilitating our productivity.

WHAT HAPPENS WHEN XERS HAVE NO ACCESS TO INFORMATION?

Military Situations Clarify The Need For Good Information

The military is a lot like a big corporation. If a commanding officer isn't telling us information that is important

along the way, if he isn't telling us where he wants us to be going, making the goals clear, staying within reach, or if we aren't able to keep him up on any problems or unusual events in our day to day operations, then you begin to have serious problems. You can't have an effective operation without good communication.
Officer in the U.S. Armed Forces

HOW XERS WORK AROUND INFORMATION MONOPOLIES

Managers who believe that Xers have short attention spans do not understand Xers' communication habits and learning styles. Until managers learn to communicate effectively with Xers and facilitate our on-the-job learning, they will continue to be frustrated by Xers' constant demand for information, endless questions, and insistence on relating to information in our own way. More important, Xers will continue to feel "dazed and confused" at work, circling around basic problems, wasting valuable time, and costing a lot of money, solely because we are not getting the information we need.

The Xers who speak in the first part of this chapter are ready, willing and able to do the hard learning necessary at the outset of any career, as well as the rigorous daily learning. But, Xers are prevented from doing so by managers who fail to keep open lines of communication and fail to facilitate friendly learning environments.

Xers told me about managers who hide information, hoard it, don't know it, don't have time to share it, or don't know how to teach it; managers who are keeping Xers in the dark—purposely, unwittingly, or in spite of themselves; managers who either can't or won't make information available to Xers, guide Xers, teach Xers, or even answer Xers' questions; managers who make it nearly impossible for Xers to learn and then complain that we have short attention spans and are not rigorous enough to teach ourselves.

When managers don't fulfill Xers' need for information, we are unable to learn and grow, less effective in our work, less satisfied and less confident that our hard work will ever pay off. That is when Xers reach for the remote control: Xers start mining the workplace for alternative sources of information, quizzing everyone from our peers to more friendly senior managers, doing our own research to the extent possible, snooping around our managers' desks if necessary.

Xers will try to change managers if we can, change jobs if we have to. Or sometimes Xers just tune out—don't care about our managers' programs anymore because we have no idea what they want anyway. One thing is for sure, Xers will never tune in to a work environment where we don't have access to information sufficient to facilitate learning and growth.

INFORMATION MONOPOLY IS ALL ABOUT POWER

Sometimes managers try to hold Xers back by actively keeping information out of Xers' reach. These managers are usually less senior, maybe a little bit threatened by ambitious Xers nipping at their heels. Many of the same Boomer managers who insist that Xers are too big for our britches and not experienced enough to fill them yet are actively preventing Xers from gaining the experience and knowledge which Xers would use to contribute valuable end-results, and perhaps surpass the value of our managers.

When managers stonewall Xers on work-related information, Xers will find ways around the wall, or under it, or over it. One Xer who speaks in the following section did what she had to—sneaking peaks at memos on her manager's chair and chatting-up her manager's secretary, just to find out what she was supposed to be doing every day on the job.

"He Would Keep Key Pieces Of Information From People"

Our manager would keep key pieces of information from people even when they needed the information to do their jobs. Even such a key point as a part of a contract that I was supposed to be negotiating. I would have to keep coming back to my manager for yes and no answers—in the middle of trying to negotiate a contract. Can you imagine that?

Rising executive at a cable television network

ARE BABY BOOMERS AFRAID THAT WITH ACCESS TO CRITICAL INFORMATION, XERS WILL PUT IT TO BETTER USE THAN OUR MANAGERS?

She Would Always Tell Me, "You Don't Need To Know"

Whenever she had a meeting or a conference call, I would ask if she wanted me to be in on the call or meeting. She would always tell me to "stay back." Or if she were preparing for something, I might ask about it and she would say, "You don't need to know." Here is where the problem would come in: A lot of times something else would come up for my manager and she would just say "cover for me" and all of this in a frantic environment while she is running around. So, I go to try to cover her obligation and then I have no answers for anyone because she would not have included me at all. She assured that I couldn't be useful in a situation like that. There might be times when some action is needed but my manager's boss can't find my manager—then she might come to me and expect me to know about what-

ever it is and be able to help. But, all I can say is "Well, I wasn't really involved with that." I hated having to say that because it makes me seem useless. They must wonder "What is she doing here all day?" And here I am working like crazy but then I look stupid because my manager won't clue me in.

Sometimes I would come in and say, "I know you're really busy but is there some way that we could meet just for a couple of minutes, so that I could know what is going on and what is expected of me?" She would usually respond that there wasn't enough time for that. When she would meet with me, we would get started and then she would interrupt constantly to answer her phone and we would never finish. I learned to go in with the goal of getting one little piece of information and would ask her very specific questions which required short answers. I kept a list of all the things I was supposed to know but didn't and whenever I got the chance I would try to get one little piece of information out of her. I had to orchestrate like mini-meetings. Then, I learned to be almost sneaky. Whenever I went in to put something on my manager's chair, I would try to quickly read all the other stuff on her chair so I could learn what was going on. So much of what I learned was from reading all the stuff on her chair. Sometimes I would go over and chat with my manager's secretary to see what she was typing, kind of glancing over her shoulder while I talked with her. It wasn't that I was nosy, it was just the only way for me to learn what I was supposed to know to do my job. When I was able to sneak some learning were the only times I was able to say something of value and contribute instead of "I don't know, I wasn't involved in that." **Assistant account executive at an advertising agency**

WHAT HAPPENS WHEN XERS ARE CUT OFF FROM INFORMATION?

Because Xers are accustomed to a complex and some-times dangerous world filled with multivalent messages from multiplicitous information sources, we have learned to lever-age information as a resource to achieve comfort and security amidst instability.

Xers need access to information in order to feel compe-tent and capable in our work. Xers are used to the informa-tion environments of mass culture and higher education— both environments in which information is abundantly avail-able. Too often, managers do not devote sufficient time and energy to creating and maintaining open information environ-ments which Xers can use as resources to maximize our effectiveness.

When Xers do not have access to open information environments, we find ourselves treading water in sink or swim environments in which we have insufficient guidance resources to match the level of responsibility we are expected to fulfill.

A Tremendous Need To Ask For Directions

It is like they are saying, "Here take it, you're on your own." Imagine being in your car on a road, knowing your intended destination...the address, knowing vaguely how to get there, but not knowing what is between here and there. You know none of the right turns and none of the landmarks and you're having a tremendous need to ask for directions. Now, imagine you are in that situation, but your passenger has been down this road a million times, knows the directions by heart, knows every landmark. But he won't share any of that information. And he yells at you every time you make a wrong turn or even pause to think about it for too long. A little help would make

my work efficient instead of a struggle.
Associate at a large law firm

"Call A Doctor"

We were left alone in the VA hospital on our first day. I remember that there was a very sick patient and an orderly came in to get me. The patient was clearly dying and the orderly said to me, "What should we do?" I said, "Call a doctor." It was my very first day being a doctor.
Physician in first year internship

Xers Need Guidance So We Don't Waste Time

The problem is that I had to be almost entirely self taught. I hardly got anything in the way of professional mentoring. I really was never taught anything. As an employee you have to take the initiative to learn. But, I think that I would have been a whole lot more effective in my job if I had gotten more guidance earlier on. I would have wasted less time. I would have been a more efficient employee and focused my skill better. There were times when I would try to approach something, and it wouldn't come out right because I didn't even fully understand the question. I don't recall someone ever saying to me, "This is how you might want to do something differently, or this is good in the following ways and bad in the following ways."
Researcher at a major television network

XERS NEED ABUNDANT INFORMATION TO LEARN EFFECTIVELY

Don't Count On Sink-or-Swim Tests

I came into the company not knowing anything about the industry. We had very limited training. They threw us in and we had to struggle just to stay afloat. Not only was the training poor, but our manager never let us know if we were doing well, if we were doing things right, so I was sort of winging it.

Loan specialist in a mortgage bank

Avoid Burning Energy Without Creating Value—And Don't Just Grunt

By and large I am a ship on a large ocean and there is no one else out there. But, you see, I am not in sales, where you get what you produce. I have a need for help, for participation in a group format, for guidance. Without guidance and a game plan and support, it is possible to burn up tons of energy, groping through annual reports every day, without creating value. My usual conversation with my manager lasts about a minute and a half. Usually it involves me walking in there, making a small statement, and he will turn around and grunt or make some kind of other noise to indicate his disposition. I have no idea if the projects I am working on are considered a positive thing.

Equity researcher at a small retail brokerage house

THROWING XERS INTO A SINK-OR-SWIM ENVIRONMENT WITHOUT INFORMATION IS LIKE THROWING US INTO AN EMPTY POOL—WE NEITHER SINK NOR SWIM, WE JUST CRASH

A Case Of Not Knowing What Was Expected

I was given a lot of freedom but not a lot of direction. So I floundered around. I only saw my research director about once a month. I spent a lot of time wasting time looking for things. I rediscovered the wheel a couple of times. For me it was a case of not knowing what was

expected of me. I thought it was going to be like school where they were going to teach me things, but it wasn't. They just threw me in. There wasn't a lot of personal support, just pressure to get results.
Chemist at a major research university

Weighty Responsibilities Require Information Flow

The problem was that for the most part I was being given way too much responsibility and no guidance. I felt all the time that I was kind of fudging it and covering for both of us. I would have to corner him and figure out what was going on. I would have to kind of joke with him and say "Okay you've got to let me know what's going on here." There was a lot of resentment. I hated him. I was caught holding the bag so many times. Eventually, I just stopped caring. I hated him. He treated his employees and his clients terribly. I mean, I was always holding the bag for him, and I hated him, so I didn't care after awhile.
Paralegal

WHEN XERS HAVE TO FAKE IT, QUALITY SUFFERS

What happens when Xers' work goals are not made clear?

Some managers give Xers only the vaguest instructions at the outset of complex assignments, even though the managers are quite picky about the details of the final product they expect. Managers who give unclear direction to Xers also have a tendency to change their minds about work-goals and repeatedly refine their initially vague instructions by critiquing round after round after round of drafts. With each new draft, Xers walk away mumbling "Why didn't you say so in the first place?"

When managers develop Xers' work-goals through this kind of revision process, they seize control of Xers' work experience and diminish the creative opportunities available to Xers in our work. These managers are using Xers as marionettes to work out their own creative processes and heading straight down the road to the dreaded management disease—micro-management.

VAGUE INSTRUCTIONS: THE FIRST SYMPTOM OF THE DREADED MANAGEMENT DISEASE...MICRO-MANAGING

Procedure: Back And Forth Many Times

Don't get pissed off at me if you give me inadequate information when you are presenting a question to me and then I don't get you the answer you are looking for. Especially, because if I ask for more information when they are posing the question, they look at me like I am nosy or something. Instead of getting the information on the table at the outset, the standard is to go back and forth ten times, which is stupid.

Staff assistant at a big six accounting firm

MICRO-MANAGERS DON'T KNOW WHAT THEY LIKE UNTIL THEY SEE IT

A Rotten Model: General Instructions, Very Specific Expectations

When he gives me an assignment, he gives very general instructions even though he has very specific expectations. Rather than have those expectations out front, he makes his expectations increasingly clear as a project is progressing. I mean specific all the way down to the font size of the print on the report I am preparing. I find out his expectations by doing a draft and eventually when he gets around to looking at it he makes comments about every little detail: "this font is too big," or "I don't like this color," and other nit-picky things. This process goes through many rounds where he picks up new details to change or changes his own mind about something. It is a very inefficient process.

Associate in an investment bank

MANAGERS WHO GIVE VAGUE INSTRUCTIONS PROBABLY LACK CLEAR GOALS

Work Isn't A Guessing Game

One time there was a letter that I was supposed to write to the client. My manager said, "I want to see it before you send it out." I tried to find him all day. I could leave it on his chair, but then he would never get back to me. So, I would have to make this judgment: is this so important that it has to go out, with or without my manager's approval? Well, since he had said he wanted to see it first, I decided I had better wait. The next day, when he saw the letter on his chair, he said, "Why didn't you send this? The client had to have it last night. You were supposed to fax this out. What is the matter with you?" He was furious that I didn't send it. All I could say was "You told me you wanted to see it before it went out, you never got back to me, and you never told me it was so important that it had to go out last night even if you didn't okay it." So, that was the end of that part.

Then, a week later, I was in the exact same situation. I had a letter that was supposed to go out and he had left for the day. After the first experience, I decided to send it out. Of course, the next day, he sees his copy of the letter on his chair. He decided he didn't like the way I worded something and became furious again. He said, "I can't believe you sent this out without showing it to me first." How am I supposed to distinguish between those

two experiences and figure out the right thing to do in the future?
Account coordinator at an advertising agency.

HOW CAN XERS PRODUCE IF WE CAN'T ASK QUESTIONS?

Many Xers say that they have a hard time asking questions of their managers at work. They talk about managers on the run, who refuse to make time for Xers, managers who are inaccessible, unapproachable, impatient, disorganized, inconsiderate, managers jumping to conclusions, answering the phone in mid-sentence, whistling for the shoe-shine attendant, interrupting Xers, and sending Xers off in a million directions, but still ignoring our questions.

Managers who don't want to deal with Xers' questions have to remember that Xers are used to prompt responses to our questions from accommodating education professionals, information telephone lines, and computer research tools, as well as books. Xers are smart information consumers and the questions we direct to managers are probably not answerable from other information sources. That is why Xers become so frustrated when managers ignore our questions.

"If I Have Questions, They Grow Impatient"

I am not learning anything, probably not doing a competent job, and working with people who don't give a damn about me or my work product, which I find bizarre. They just assign me work and say: go do it. They should be teaching me how to do the work. I do it as best I can but if I ask questions, during an assignment, they grow upset, impatient and angry. Of course, that is frustrating and makes it hard to do a good job.
Associate at a large law firm

Haste Battles Against Clarity And Strong Information Flow

My manager doesn't give a lot of thought to what I already know, what I have learned, what I am going to have to learn. She doesn't seem to think through what I am going to learn from a project or if something is way over my head. I have to try to slow her down by asking her questions or else get information in a sort of ad hoc way from other people in the group. Just slowing her down to get a little direction can be really difficult. So I go elsewhere, to another banker, or to a peer, who might know a little bit more about something.

Associate at an investment bank

Focus On The People In Front Of You

This manager didn't pay attention to me when I would try to talk with him. I would be talking with him and trying to follow his eyes but they wouldn't ever focus on me and then the phone would ring and he would pick it up. I felt like I had to fight to get him to pay attention to me, to try to get him to help me with any problem. If something seemed really urgent then he would be forced to pay attention and then he usually overreacted.

Loan specialist in a mortgage bank

Rushed Answers Do More Harm Than Good

A lot of my colleagues say (my manager) gives very little direction. I would never want him as my lawyer. He delegates work to people but doesn't fulfill his responsibility to supervise. Imagine being a client and having him delegate the work to someone really junior who doesn't really know what he is doing, without some guidance. That means the work is not being done competently. There were times when I had tons of questions and I felt that I couldn't ask. If I were able to ask key questions at

the right times, it would cut down my time tremendously and make my work ten times more efficient, and if they really have a time crunch it just seems to make more sense to do that.
Associate at a large law firm

WHEN MANAGERS ARE UNAVAILABLE TO ANSWER XERS' QUESTIONS, THEY SLOW DOWN XERS' PRODUCTIVITY

Scattered Doesn't Equal Busy

The first manager I had was everywhere, very disorganized, never on time. It was frustrating because it felt like this guy never had the time to give, the time that I deserved. In the beginning it was the worst because that is when I really needed training and support. Being new and having to deal with people who had been in the business for thirty years was difficult enough and then to have no access, no way to ask questions was terrible.
Insurance underwriter

MANAGERS WHO TREAT XERS' QUESTIONS AS TRIVIAL SEND THE MESSAGE THAT OUR WORK MUST BE TRIVIAL TOO

Avoid Seeming Too Important To Approach

I have been told, "Don't approach this partner with trivial questions, he is too busy." I have had barely any interaction with him at all and I don't know if I care to. How am I supposed to know what is too trivial for him? The junior associates will talk with each other to try to find out if the partner is in a good mood. The funny thing is that he is just down the hall—but he is just not accessible. I always have to wonder if it is the right time to ask a question. Sometimes I am made to feel that I have asked

an unnecessary question, that I should have figured it out on my own. Even sometimes when it is a question of judgment which I really couldn't look up in a book.
Associate in a mid-sized law firm

"I Don't Have Time For That Right Now"

My manager always has some other place to be. "I just don't have time for that right now." Or "You're right to mention that but that's a can of worms. Good, okay, here are the things we need to talk about right now—a, b, c, d." Then with a minute left, he will say, "Is there anything else?" If I mention something he doesn't want to talk about, he just says there isn't enough time. "Good seeing you, don't have time for that right now." This is the "too busy tactic."
Senior staffer in a non-profit foundation

TOO OFTEN, XERS HAVE TO GO AHEAD AND DO OUR JOBS WITHOUT THE ANSWERS WE NEED

"He Doesn't Know How To Listen To People"

I think he is a good lawyer, but as a manager he is uncomfortable around people. He is very short, tense, ill at ease. He doesn't listen and will cut me off in mid-sentence. One time I had to talk with him about prioritizing two projects I was working on. He got very impatient and just came to conclusions and I had to correct him and tell him that the conclusions he was drawing were wrong. He wasn't really listening to what I was saying, but coming to conclusions because he was too impatient, so I never got my questions on the table. I went to another colleague to talk about it and she told me not to take anything he says personally. Actually, a lot of people have told me that. I don't think he is mean, I just

think he doesn't know how to listen to people.
**Assistant corporation counsel in law department of a
major city**

WHEN MANAGERS TREAT XERS' QUESTIONS AS INVITATIONS TO ABUSE US, MANAGERS LOSE XERS' RESPECT

Insulting Underlings Undermines Credibility

*One time, I needed to ask some questions of a manager
in my group. I went into his office, sat down, asked a
question, he picked up a phone call, I asked him again,
he picked up the phone. I asked again, he picked up the
phone again. He put down the phone and whistled for
the shoe-shine boy. This manager was going to get his
shoes shined in front of me. To be expected to watch
him get his shoes shined while I am talking with him was
so degrading—degrading for the shoe-shine boy, degrading for me and so pompous of him. I felt like it was
unprofessional and it made me very angry. It may have
been a wasted gesture, but I got up and left. No way was
I going to sit there and watch this guy get his shoes
shined. I don't even think he noticed.*
Analyst at an investment bank

BY PROVIDING XERS WITH ACCESS TO OUR MOST RELIABLE PROBLEM SOLVING RESOURCE, MANAGERS CAN MAXIMIZE XERS' RELATIONSHIP TO INFORMATION

Managers who understand Xers' relationship with information are best able to support atmospheres of learning and
growth, facilitating Xers' happiness, productivity, and innovation. While Xers' great comfort level with technology is critical
to our value in the workplace of the future, engaging Xers'
unique style of communicating and learning is critical to

managers' ability to maximize Xers' value. In the right information environment, Xers' ability quickly to evaluate and assimilate massive quantities of information from multiple sources is our greatest strength.

Because Xers are accustomed to technology which provides information in massive quantities, in diverse formats, and represents a wide range of differing perspectives, we operate best in information environments which mirror that experience.

The best way to maximize Xers' special relationship with information is to allow Xers the freedom to access and process, at our own pace, information from multiple sources in abundant quantity and diverse formats.

Information environments, conditioned by optimal access and open communication, make Xers feel secure, competent, powerful, and creative in our work. Because this kind of environment cultivates Xers' unique style, instead of trying to squelch it, Xers are more efficient and productive, develop respect for our managers as teachers, are more willing to work harder for them, and more able to work better for them.

HOW DO GOOD MANAGERS KEEP XERS INFORMED?

Xers are very effective consumers of information when managers make sufficient information resources available to us. The Xers in this section talk about managers who are effective at keeping Xers informed by setting clear goals and maintaining open lines of communication.

Xers describe managers who provide information through regular meetings where managers review projects with Xers in order to keep us up to speed on the latest managerial developments, set weekly goals and track results in order to refine projects, answer questions and resolve problems. By all of these means, effective managers are keeping Xers informed with easy access to steady streams of information—accessible like channels at the touch of a remote control. The result is Xers who are confident, efficient, productive, and creative.

Spend The Time To Bring Your Staff Up To Speed

Our staff meetings are great too. They go through all of the projects and there is a lot of room for questions. They spend the time to bring the staff up to speed. That means we all know what is going on and we are all devoted to making things happen the way our manager wants.

Analyst in a small investment bank

Regular Meetings Should Be Brief And Detail-Oriented

The firm has a "results meeting" every Monday morning. We discuss the results achieved for each client the previous week. Immediately after the results meeting, I meet with my manager to plan our own agenda for the coming week. We keep identical notebooks with headings for each client on a separate page and the specific tasks that are to be accomplished by each of us for each client. We arrive at the list by reviewing the previous week's list together, seeing what each one of us has accomplished, what needs follow up and then we set the agenda of new tasks for each client.

Junior account executive at a mid-sized PR firm

"He Will Take The Time To Talk With Me"

I feel at any time I can go into his office. Even if it isn't the most important thing to him, he will take the time to talk with me. With short little meetings, people solve their problems. There is no line. I can call him at home. It's quite clear that he is the boss, but you feel he is on your side.

Admissions director for a non-profit educational organization

Tell Xers Why We Are Doing What We Are Doing

She was a good manager, because she was good about telling me why I was doing what I was doing. I was making formula samples with very small variations between them. Knowing what the company was trying to determine made me much more interested in the results.

Chemical technician in development lab of major food company

Wasted Hours Are Hard To Bill Or Write Off

The styles of the managers at my new job made it possible to ask questions and get the necessary information. They always kept me up on what we were doing and why and were available if I needed some guidance. My first month I made about 250 billable hours, which is a lot, I wrote a lot tighter memos than before, my analysis was much better, and I could feel myself learning a lot more. I was much more productive than I had been and I wasn't wasting hours so that they didn't have to be written off when it came time to bill the client.

Associate at a large law firm

WHAT IS THE TEACHING PART OF MANAGING XERS?

Xers spoke with admiration and affection about managers who recognize that teaching Xers is a critical element of effectively managing our work.

The most effective managers devote substantial time and energy to teaching Xers, sharing expertise and investing in Xers by actively improving our knowledge and skill bases. They go beyond providing Xers with the information resources which we need to do our jobs. Managers who actively teach Xers on the job are demonstrating their commitment to helping Xers build our own personal assets for the future— teaching is the most effective vehicle by which managers can participate directly in Xers' self-building. Teaching managers recognize that.

Although the primary learning resource available to and utilized by Xers is an endless stream of information, teachers have always been our primary human supporters outside of family (and sometimes including family). Xers rarely turn to managers for raw information—rather Xers want to learn, from managers, knowledge which is available from no other source.

Because we do not yet have many years of professional experience, Xers are thrilled when teaching managers make available to us their own high level professional judgment. With that additional learning, Xers are that much more equipped to bring our creative energy to bear on problems. Xers are even willing to let teaching managers help us focus our informational inquiries, when managers have demonstrated their commitment to our learning and growth.

In this section, Xers describe managers who are investing time and energy in teaching Xers, listening to our questions, providing answers and insights, and knowledge which we cannot hope to find elsewhere. By helping Xers to add judgment and seasoning to our learning process, teaching managers help Xers to accelerate our knowledge and skills, and continue to improve our work-repertoires at a faster pace.

This is why teaching managers win Xers' deepest respect and loyalty, as well as our most diligent efforts. By teaching, managers are investing wisely. The more Xers learn, the more capable, independent, and effective Xers become—the more valuable Xers can be, not only to ourselves, but also to our managers.

Foster A Basic Willingness To Share

The biggest thing I get out of it is that my manager is a superstar in his field and he is willing to share that with me. He is completely wrapped up in the industry and he is an expert and he is willing to be a teacher. We are very high on ourselves, the group, and charged up because of that.

Business development manager in a cable television network

"He Spent A Lot Of Time Making Sure I Understood"

My manager worked very closely with me, like personal tutoring on the job. He spent time making sure that I understood things. The more I learned and the more my ability grew, the more he let me take responsibility. Every time I had a question I would ask and he would take the time to explain, not superficially. I was able to learn a lot by working very closely and observing. It was a good feeling. I felt like part of the team and like anything I did was a contribution. It made me want to take more and more responsibility and work hard for this company. Everybody was on board.

Planning department associate at a major car company

Xers Admire Managers Who Can Explain

There is one partner I admire because he can explain a problem in simple and understandable terms. He is very articulate, speaks slowly and clearly and seems to comprehend what an associate at my level might have been exposed to at this point in my career. First of all, he tells me clearly what he wants. He will listen to any questions I have about an assignment. He is generally approachable for further questions. He is also willing to admit that he may not fully understand something, which shows me that he is still human. He will also ask me in a case like that if maybe I can help him understand.

Associate at a large law firm

TEACHING MANAGERS CAN BECOME XERS' PRIMARY HUMAN SUPPORTERS

"The Things She Says To Me Really Stick"

My new manager is someone I think of as a mentor and someone who can teach me a lot. She is very demanding, but she is very willing to let me express my views and she pushes me to ask questions. If she is telling me something and I am nodding, she will stop and ask me "Are you sure you understand what I just said?" She is able to size up when I am struggling, when she needs to check in with me and help me understand. She always takes the time to spell things out, not in a condescending way, but in a way that is intended to make sure I genuinely understand. The things she says to me really stick. She has my respect and I gladly work hard for her.

Research assistant in a public interest organization

No Sense Of Hierarchy But A Real Sense Of Authority

Upon my arrival, I was assigned a mentor and then four students who needed remedial tutoring. Using the students as a lab, I honed my teaching skills. Then for an hour a day I discussed the teaching with my mentor and we used the teaching as a point of reflection. That lasted for about eight weeks and it made me feel terrific. This guy was a real pro, deeply committed, superb at his craft. What made me feel so positive was that there was no sense of hierarchy. Although, there was a real sense of his authority. He didn't have to rely on hierarchy. His manner radiated authority and he manifested excellence and it made me and others want to respect him and want to work hard for him. There was something inspirational about it.

High school teacher

MANAGERS TEACHING SKILLS - XERS RESPONSIBLE FOR THE SKILLS x INFINITY

"The Next Time, I Would Solve That Problem"

There was one manager who was the best manager I have ever had anywhere. He was smart, he really knew what he was talking about, he cared and was very compassionate about the people that worked for him. One night, I was at work at about 10 p.m. and I had been there beating my head against the wall for at least a couple of hours, working on a bear of a problem. It was during game two of the NBA finals and I remember it well because I had to miss that game because I was working so hard. He knew I was a big basketball fan. This manager was great. He pulled up a chair and we talked a little bit about the basketball game we were missing. Then he said, "Let's see if we can get past this problem," and we worked on it together for about an hour and we finally got it. He dug right into it with me and we got it worked out together and he showed me how to deal with that kind of problem. That experience told me a lot about this manager and it tells you a lot about him. He was a real teacher. He knew that the next time that problem came up, I would be the guy to solve it.

Information systems consultant

CHAPTER 7:

Space And Time— Maximizing Xers' Creative Prowess

THIS GENERATION'S CREATIVE BENT

Most people thrive on creative expression. So, what is unique about the creative predisposition of Generation X? Xers' investment in our creative faculties is closely linked to our quest for self-building in our lives and careers. Look at Xers' innovative nature in the spotlight of our personal profile.

Well versed in the reality of our personal vulnerability to forces great and small, nurtured on the technology of information revolution, schooled on a rapid stream of diverse messages, experienced in the art of solitary problem solving, Xers are conditioned to sort and evaluate information quickly, define and solve problems independently, take creative risks, and seek safety in innovation.

Xers cautiously maneuver toward oases of firm ground, resolute in our self-reliance, determined to learn and grow, to develop ourselves and our abilities. We want to benefit ourselves by making meaningful contributions to institutions which value our work, to steadily increase our own value as entrepreneurs of our own creative abilities. And we want to build—build within ourselves a new form of career security, build from within ourselves a safer future for our generation and the generations which follow us.

For Xers, our creative abilities make up the critical tool-kit with which we navigate safely in the world. Our creative ability is also Xers' primary asset for investing in our careers—by creating valuable end-products, Xers hope to demonstrate our abilities in order to gain increasing responsibility and greater opportunities to create. When Xers are free to pursue this form of creative investment, the result is an upward spiral of innovation and productivity.

Xers function best when managed as responsible independent creative forces—free to take risks, to make mistakes, to try our own solutions. Managers who are able to facilitate Xers' process of creative investment will benefit, not only from Xers' increased motivation and commitment, but also from the fruits of Xers' innovation.

Xers offer a unique creative prowess, which holds great value for managers. Because of Xers' facility with information, Xers' lightning fast ability to sort and file multiplicitous messages from multiple sources, because Xers are adaptable like chameleons and able to operate in new and different environments, Xers see new connections where prior generations see confusion and noise. Where others see problems, Xers see possibilities. Xers' creative prowess is energized by opportunities to define and solve problems—to challenge ourselves in our own space and time.

RULE OF X: THERE ARE NO PROBLEMS, ONLY PROJECTS

Providing working space is the best way managers can

cater to Xers' independence and encourage our natural innovation. In order to best understand the concept of working space, managers should think in very physical terms— space is less a concept than an actual physical distance between managers and Xers' daily work goals, physical distance which opens up a critical proprietary work terrain for Xers.

Using very few materials and tools, managers can build around Xers' creative process a palpable space which facilitates our greatest productivity. The materials necessary to build work space are readily available—goals, responsibility, absence, and information.

Xers must be given clear goals in the form of responsibility for tangible end-products. The clarity of goal setting requires more, however, than a strict definition of the end-product. The most important clarity relates to ownership of goals—making plain distinctions between which tangible end results belong to Xers as opposed to those which belong to managers.

Often, achieving this clarity necessitates the early dissection of projects into more clearly delineated segments—a management tool which is, in itself, altogether useful. Needless to say, as projects evolve, the priority level of certain intermediate end-results will fluctuate.

That's fine—Xers are ready to adapt quickly and effortlessly to sudden change. We will handle responsibilities minor or major, create results final, intermediate or preliminary—as long as our own end-goals are clear. By consistently defining the ownership of end-results in demand at each phase of a project, managers ensure that Xers know with certainty which end-results are within our power to produce. By fitting goals and responsibility together like puzzle pieces, managers successfully assemble the foundation of Xers' work space.

Upon that foundation, managers need to balance the remaining elements—absence and information. Managers can strengthen Xers' working space between goal-setting and deadlines by maintaining a disciplined absence from that space. Xers are glad to follow directions, stay within parameters, adhere to guidelines, and meet specifications. Whatever the limits to our work space, Xers need to have one hundred percent responsibility for the end-result encompassed by that space.

But Xers' work space is not lonely. Remember, the final element is our most reliable problem-solving resource, our constant sustenance—information.

MANAGERS WHO LET XERS WORK ON OUR OWN TERRAIN, ENJOY THE FRUITS OF OUR ENTREPRENEURIAL SPIRIT

In order to complete the construction of Xers' ideal work space, managers need to make sure that Xers can access maximum information from within that space.

The first, more obvious step is to make available to Xers every informational resource possible—print sources, on-line sources and human sources. Given the resources, Xers will set our own pace of information gathering and learning—on an as needed basis.

The second, more difficult step, is for managers to balance their own absence with Xers' periodic need to gain information directly from our managers—we are likely to ask questions and seek input. Should managers play hard to get? Is that part of the absence that is necessary to Xers' work space? When managers start playing coy, they signal to Xers that they are not serious about our self-building—they make clear that they have no potential as teaching managers and they begin to lose credibility.

Managers serious about building access to information into Xers' work space can follow a simple rule—let Xers seek you out. Don't seek out Xers—leave the seeking to us. When managers allow Xers to set the pace of management interactions, they see quickly that Xers only approach managers with very acute queries—always seeking information which is unavailable from any other source.

Managers who listen carefully to Xers' queries are able to respond acutely without invading Xers' space—answering only the questions Xers ask and allowing Xers to disappear peacefully when we are ready to return to our space.

Managers who fit together the elements of responsibility, goals, absence and information and successfully assemble ideal work space for Xers, will benefit from Xers most innovative efforts. Xers work our hearts out for managers who offer responsibility for end-results and the corresponding freedom to achieve those results, managers who challenge Xers and give us the day-to-day decision-making power that makes our creativity possible.

Managers who give Xers the space to focus on creative solutions, take risks and make mistakes, invent new approaches, and reap benefits in terms of self-building and personal security will succeed with Generation X. Those managers can harness Xers' entrepreneurial spirit and achieve end-results that go straight to the bottom line.

THE PARADOX OF MANAGING XERS: DELEGATION IS THE BEST HARNESS OF SKILLS

"I Do Better Work If I Am Able To Do It My Way"

I have a lot of respect for my manager because he is very precise about what he wants but very flexible about how he lets me get there. He might say to me "Here is where we are on a particular situation. We want to get to point X. The information we need is A, B, C. Here is why I want to look at it. Now go put that together by Z date." That gives me a little more freedom to approach the project. It is positive because I like to do things my way and I am producing much better work here than I would under different circumstances.

Head of circulation for a magazine holding company

"He Lets Me Do The Job He Hired Me To Do"

My manager doesn't lean over my shoulder wanting to know what I am doing every minute of every day. It is very clear what I have to produce, and my manager trusts me to be professional in getting my results. He lets me do the job which he hired me to do, lets me make the day to day decisions that I need to make, and doesn't try to baby-sit me. That gives me room to do my work the way I want to do it, it means that I am approaching things my own way and that makes me a whole lot more productive.

Business development manager for a large consumer products company

Let Xers Carry Our Own Responsibilities

The up side is that the managers are willing to let us carry our own responsibilities. We have guidelines that we work within, but other than that, I can decide how to meet my responsibilities. I can go weeks at a time without ever having to talk to my managers as long as I am doing my job and performing well. That way I am on my own, doing my own thing and I am able to focus on results. I know what the bottom line is going to be and it is up to me to get there however I see fit.

Marketing executive for a manufacturer of commercial goods

RULE OF X: IN RESPONSIBILITY, XERS FIND ALL THE WORKING SPACE WE NEED

"I Respect It Because It Is My Responsibility"

Each day, I am responsible for checking a certain trading device and the whole group relies on me for this. This is a daily responsibility that is all mine. If I don't do it every day and something is overlooked, we could lose hundreds of thousands of dollars very quickly. The reward is knowing that there are a lot of pitfalls and mistakes to be made, but that I am patient enough to get through the maze each time. I respect the task because it is my responsibility and, even though there is a lot of room to screw up, it is something that I have never once screwed up.

Portfolio assistant in a large commercial bank

Give Xers Our "Own Little Businesses"

I am working out of a home office now. Overall it is like having my own little business. In my situation, I have weekly goals and I have a weekly report due. I type that up and fax it to my manager each Monday morning. As long as I am meeting my weekly goals, then I can spend my time getting the job done however I want to, instead of focusing on all the distractions in the corporate headquarters. In my little home office, I call the shots.

National account manager for a major consumer products company

"If Something Isn't Working, I Am Free To Switch"

I have a lot of freedom to do what I want within the bounds of the curriculum. I like to plan my own lessons. It improves the quality of my interactions with the kids because I am not forced to teach them in a certain way. If something isn't working I am free to switch to do something else. That is the thing that keeps me interested in the job. Teaching, for me, is all about trying in any way I can think of, something new, to get across the material to the kids.

High school science teacher

"I Could Do What I Needed...And Make My Manager Look Good"

With more responsibility, I was getting more support from my manager and that was allowing me to grow in the company and contribute more. I have been able to move up in the company because my manager has been very supportive in letting me shape my job. He gave me opportunities to be more independent when I sought them. If I came up with a solution to a problem or an innovative idea, I could move on it myself. In this environment, I could do what I needed to do and make my manager look good at the same time.

Marketing coordinator for a publishing company

WORKING SPACE IS THE ANTIDOTE TO MICRO-MANAGEMENT

The Xers who speak in this section describe managers who set clear deadlines for the achievement of tangible end-products and provide the information and resources Xers need to achieve results at our own pace. In between goal-setting and deadlines, these managers are letting Xers set the frequency of interaction between them, unless something unusual comes up. Letting Xers manage our own time and set our own schedules is part of managing Xers as responsible and independent creative forces.

When managers support Xers' independence by allowing us the freedom to schedule our own work time, Xers are willing to devote more time to work. Most managers will find that Xers working at our own pace cover a lot more ground in a lot less time than we would if our managers controlled our every minute.

"I Can Manage My Own Time"

The manager sets an agenda at the first meeting and sets a series of dates by which certain goals have to be met. Other than that, we are left alone to decide on the specifics of the general problem. In between these dates, unless I want it and seek it out, I don't have to see my manager at all. I know what I need to do within a certain date and I can manage my time any way I want, as long as I deliver what it is that I am responsible to deliver. That means I can approach problems in a way that brings out my best work.
Consultant at a business consulting company

Xers Are Effective Consumers Of Time

I like the job because there is quite a bit of freedom in terms of setting my own schedule. I appreciate that a lot because I am responsible and it is nice to be trusted enough to do my job. I feel good not having to punch in. It's a more comfortable way for me to work and it makes me a more independent entity in the company. I am expected to close a certain number of loans and when it is busy, I am here as late as I need to be. What works well for me is that I can make these determinations and I can decide when to be here working at the times when I am going to be most productive. If I am super busy, it only makes sense for me to be working when I can produce at an efficient pace.
Loan specialist in a mortgage brokerage house

"It Is Kind Of An Honor System"

The job is flexible in terms of taking time off and switching hours. You can come in when you want, just as long as you do your work. It is kind of an honor system and people are expected to put in their time, especially since the management is so cool about trusting us to do the work. It gives me the flexibility to attend to certain things in my life when it works best for me, which makes me feel a lot better about being at work when I am here. I put in more time if anything, but I also choose when I am going to be here. That means I want to be at work when I am here and that means I feel a lot better about my job. I feel like they are trusting us and they are flexible in the face of people's different scheduling needs. There is a lot of mutual respect because of that.
Researcher in an investment information service

Encourage Xers To Create 80 Percent Of The Value In 20 Percent Of The Time

At this firm they say "80/20." That means if you can do 80 percent of the value in 20 percent of the time, do it. The critical thing is what we deliver to the client. Internally, people are respected here for being able to do their work and get out of here. That means if I can solve my problems and produce, I am done. You can bet that no one is cutting corners to get the job done faster. It just means that there is a real incentive to work efficiently when you are working. The bottom line is the product, not the time.
Associate at an investment bank

"I Can Hang A Sign Out That Says 'Gone Fishing'"

My current manager gives me my goals for what I am going to produce, and then he leaves me alone. If I produce a weekly goal in a day, a monthly goal in a week, a yearly goal in a month, I can hang a sign out that says "gone fishing." It is an incentive to produce and it makes me feel like the time is mine, like I am my own boss. And, it's a whole lot better working for yourself than working for someone else.

National account manager for a major consumer products company

SMART MANAGERS LEAVE XERS IN CONTROL OF OUR OWN TIME WHILE STILL MANAGING OUR WORK

Xers are natural problem solvers because we are used to confronting personal challenges as sole proprietors. Indeed, Xers' problem solving ability is key to our self-definition and pride—the primary focus of our entrepreneurism is generating regular proof to others and confirmation to ourselves that our creative abilities are growing in value.

Given sufficient access to information and full responsibility to find solutions, Xers will look at most any problem as an opportunity to succeed. Because Xers seek to invest by making valuable contributions in the form of end-results, every problem we are able to solve and every result we are able to produce is an investment opportunity.

The Xers who speak in this section describe managers who are availing themselves and their companies of Xers' tremendous innovative power, trusting Xers to define problems and pursue creative solutions, take risks and make mistakes, stretch limits and improvise. When managers allow Xers to express ourselves in our work, they reap the benefits of Xers' most excited, diligent, dexterous and innovative problem solving.

"I'm Not Afraid Of Making A Mistake"

The key factor in my success has been my manager's trust in my competence, enough trust back and forth that it is understood that sometimes I might make a mistake. I am not afraid to act because I'm not afraid of making a mistake. I am often coming up with solutions to age old problems that no one here would ever have thought to try.

Program assistant for a nonprofit foundation

PROBLEM + INFORMATION + SPACE + TIME - XER INNOVATION

Support Creativity With An Atmosphere Of Trust

I knew my manager had confidence in me and he trusted my judgment and gave me a lot of responsibility. He would take my word, rather than check up on me all the time. That let me know that I was valued and trusted. This kind of trust from a manager affects my work very positively because it means I don't second guess myself all the time. Knowing my manager trusts my judgment gives me the confidence to look at things a little differently and try something new and that increases my creative output.

Marketing coordinator for a publishing company

The Biggest Motivator For A Problem Solver: The Problem Itself

If I am going to put together a good report for a client, I need the freedom to improvise. If I do something new that works, my portfolio manager is going to love that and I get the enjoyment of knowing that I did some creative work on my own and it was appreciated. That can be a factor in having a client bring more money into the bank, which is helping out the whole group and the

*bank and that is good for everyone. When I have room to
improvise in solving problems for clients, that is when I
do my best work.*
Portfolio assistant in a large commercial bank

Let Xers Define Problems So We Can Create Solutions

*We are crunching the numbers and to the extent pos-
sible we are left alone. I think that we are so different
they don't understand what we do. We have a bottom
line like everybody else. Our manager is checking with
us constantly, not ruthlessly, just making sure we stay on
track. He tells us what to do but he tries to give us
creative freedom because when we are left alone we
tend to come up with some of the most lucrative new
trading strategies or computer models.*

*Physicists have been coming to Wall Street for about ten
years. We think that it is kind of like nerd revenge.*
**Physics Ph.D. building computer models for a major
investment bank**

"It Is Visionary, Strategic"

*I feel like I am creating my own business, because we
are creating it from scratch. I am doing the analysis,
coming up with the questions and the answers. I am
writing the proposal that will be made to senior management. There is a lot of responsibility and this project is
going to take up a lot of my time in the future. If feels
good because it is very new and I am a driving force. It is
very satisfying to make recommendations and see them
included. I am creating the vision in many ways. This is
the most rewarding part of my job by far. I prioritize this
project because I have the most responsibility, because
it is more interesting, it is visionary, strategic.*
Marketing manager for a major financial services firm

OWNERSHIP OF RESULTS MEANS INTENSE COMMITMENT

Xers' most tangible form of investment is the end-product. Because creative prowess is the cornerstone of Xers' self-image, our end-products are extensions of ourselves—the value of our end-products is a reflection of our own value and our ability to create value. In tangible end-products, Xers demonstrate our abilities, leave behind proof that our work is valuable, and confirm that value for ourselves.

Xers' creative expression and the products of that expression form a proving ground for our entire self-building process.

In our individual successes, Xers are able to experience the progress of our quest to find security in our own creative prowess. The significance of that experience can be felt in the words of the Xers who speak in the following section. Managers who successfully facilitate for Xers the ultimate expression of our self-building process provide Xers with a meaningful and life affirming work experience. These managers also benefit from the valuable fruits of Xers' self-expression.

The Exhilaration Of The Job Itself

You have to derive satisfaction from the work itself because it is so trying and so stressful. But, the power and skill that it takes to be in the operating room, to cut into people, to be in the emergency room setting a fracture—it takes focus and concentration and physical stamina as much as skill. And the reward is really just seeing my patients get better, seeing the operation work, seeing that the skills and training that I have worked so hard to develop can actually make people better. That is an absolute thrill. To have the skill and the privilege to cure people is like, "Hey, I'm a doctor, I'm allowed to cut

*into people and fix them." That is really the biggest
reward.*
Physician in surgical residency

Xers Want To Create Distinction

*It was great to be creating something that had my own
kind of signature. The part of the job that I loved was
writing for the company newsletter. I got to choose what
I was going to write about in the newsletter and it was
my own project. That was definitely the project which got
my special effort. For me, seeing that article in print in
every newsletter was definitely the highlight of my job.*
Researcher in an investment information service

"The Decision That Goes Out Is Basically Mine"

*This is one of the few jobs where my opinion really
counts. My manager is responsible for the ultimate
decision of the agency but he takes his cues from me.
That gives me a lot of power and has a big impact on the
way I approach my work. I am creating the final product—the decision that goes out of this agency is basically
mine. I take real pride in the decisions and I work hard
enough to make sure my decisions are better than the
vast majority of decisions that come out of this agency.*
Official in a federal agency in Washington

Xers Seek "The Incredible Freedom To Be Creative"

*There was the rare opportunity to go to the Congressman
with an idea for a bill and he might say to go write the
bill. I got to do that a few times and that was an incredible experience, having an opportunity to write a law, to
influence the law that directly. That just felt like such
incredible creative freedom—I worked with a lot more
intensity on those projects than anything else by far. I*

would follow the bill all the way to the floor if it got that far. Those kinds of opportunities, to be making my own legislation, that alone made the job worthwhile.
Legislative assistant in a congressional office

CHAPTER 8:

Bringing Out The Best In Generation X

XERS ARE A GROWING PHENOMENON

The stakes in Managing Generation X are no less than the economic future of a nation and the talents of an entire generation. Xers will dominate the workplace of the future. Our prominence continues to grow as we assume increasingly critical positions—already preparing to be the managers of tomorrow.

In not too long, Xers will inherit control of the companies which Baby Boomers are inheriting today. This is a good thing. We are perfectly suited to the workplace of the future because of our comfort level with technology and our adaptability to change. The best managers see this trend and take advantage of it.

Doubting Boomers should ponder the coups in which they are now ousting their own forerunners on corporate boards and executive committees all over the land. If Boomer managers don't learn how to manage Xers effectively, the confused looks of anachronism in the corporate board rooms may soon be their own. But, there is much more at stake than who will sit on tomorrow's boards of directors because Xers produce a lot of what managers are selling today. Managed well, Xers add great value to today's bottom line—value that is squandered by managers who insist on writing off Xers' management needs.

DON'T BUY INTO EASY STEREOTYPES

Many of the managers described in this book mismanage Xers because they operate under fundamental misconceptions about the character of our generation. They fail to recognize that the challenge of managing Xers involves unique generational needs and expectations. As a consequence of their failure to understand our needs and expectations, these managers undervalue Xers and disqualify themselves from our personal investment portfolios—the failure of understanding leads directly to a loss of value at the bottom line.

Because they misinterpret Xers' quest for firm ground as the manifestation of unwieldy and unrealistic ambition, these managers have no idea how to motivate Xers. Unable to understand Xers' perspective on the concept of traditional dues paying, these managers are unable to imagine the new bargain Xers are willing to negotiate—Xers' short-term investments in the form of valuable end-results in exchange for dividends which contribute to our pursuit of a new self-based career security.

Misunderstanding Xers' natural skepticism of institutional relationships and our cautious investment posture, these managers assume that Xers are disloyal by nature. They dismiss the possibility of building corporate cultures in which

Xers are made to feel welcome. Unaware of the significance of Xers' unique style of communication and learning, these managers are simply not prepared to supply Xers with the information resources we require, leaving Xers feeling under-resourced and insecure.

Because they do not understand Xers' creative entrepreneurism, these managers are unable to build around Xers the right kind of working space and time to facilitate the creation of tangible end-products. These managers are underutilizing the valuable resource of Generation X—robbing themselves and their companies' bottom lines of Xers' commitment and talent. They also rob Xers of wonderful opportunities for self-building—and they rob society of the inestimable value of Xers' countless potential innovations.

A NEW UNDERSTANDING OF A NEW PROFILE

Can this book help managers understand the particular needs and expectations of Generation X? Enough to help managers rise to the challenge of maximizing Xers' talents to the mutual benefit of all concerned? Enough to start bringing out the best in Generation X?

By offering a new understanding of Xers' history, this book aims to promote a new profile of Generation X, a reinterpretation of our generational character, new promise for the future we are destined to lead, and a new perspective from which to manage Xers in the workplace.

Rest assured, Xers are not a generation of disloyal disinterested cynical slackers—the myth has got to die. Those who hold onto the myth will lose the future. Far from being apathetic about work, Xers see our work and careers as fundamental to our self-definition.

The primary challenge Xers face in our careers is the search for a new form of career security to replace the outmoded concept of long-term job security with one employer.

Managers who understand Xers for who we are can interpret our behavior and our potential. They know that Xers' career driven quest for personal security presents a historic management opportunity. Xers are uniquely suited to the workplace of the future. Our innovative power is the key to unlocking yet undiscovered sources of value.

Treat Generation X as a precious resource, understand our history, appreciate our style, cultivate our individuality, invest in our self-building, and contribute to an economic future in which success and safety define each other—a future in which Xers begin to achieve the new self-based career security for which we quest.

Shaped by the historic forces of atomization and information revolution, instability and rapid change, Xers are born to lead the Third Wave into the twenty-first century. Xers' self-reliant creativity is more than the character by which Xers will lead. There lie the seeds of innovation by which Xers' will ultimately realize our vision of the future.

Managers who believe in this generation need to make a commitment to manage Xers differently. Don't expect traditional dues paying from Xers. Don't expect Xers to participate in teams the same way our forerunners have. Don't expect Xers to process information the way you do, to communicate the way you do, to learn the way you do, to use technology the way you do, to utilize knowledge the way you do. Don't expect Xers to work in the same kind of space you do or the same kind of time or the same kind of culture. Don't assume that Xers won't find better approaches more appropriate to the virtual economy and virtual workplace of the future.

Commit to Xers' quest for a self-based career security. By contributing to Xers' self-building process, managers can become co-beneficiaries of our greatest creative investments. Managers can contribute to the self-building process by building corporate cultures which support the value of Xers as individuals, by valuing Xers' relationship to information and accommodating our unique style of learning and communication, by appreciating Xers' creative prowess enough to provide working space and time. Managers can facilitate Xers' entrepreneurial nature and creative spirit by making it possible for Xers to experience our work as the most powerful extension of ourselves. The benefits reside in Xers' commitment to innovation, the proof of our creative talent and confirmation of our self-worth—the very firm ground which can only reside within ourselves.

POSITIVE EXPERIENCE + OPPORTUNITIES FOR SUCCESS = XER LOYALTY

The success stories that appear throughout this book offer great promise for the future of Generation Xers in the workplace. It's encouraging to read about managers who are providing the self-building and personal security Xers seek in our careers, building corporate cultures in which Xers are eager to invest our work entrepreneurially, inspiring Xers to innovate in pursuit of management driven goals.

Successful Xers describe managers creating open information environments in which Xers can communicate effectively and learn at our own pace from multiple information resources. Thriving Xers tell of mentoring relationships with empowering managers who are challenging Xers, teaching Xers, giving Xers the room we need to express our individualism in our work, responsibility for tangible end-products and enough creative freedom to produce innovative results.

Satisfied Xers talk about managers providing meaningful status reports on job performance—concise, accurate, specific, and timely feedback.

The best managers actively participate in the building of Xers' careers by providing Xers with opportunities to advance and opportunities to lead. It is these managers from whom others can learn to bring out the best in Generation X. At our best, Xers are highly motivated, innovative, productive and determined to share the fruits of Xer creativity with the people who believe in us.

"When I Am Happy, I Work a Lot Harder"

The Chairman is very conscious of making sure that my experience is positive. He is very good about setting very clear objectives and then staying on top of it in a non-intrusive way. He has very clear and fair expectations and he has been great about guiding and supporting my career. He knows that is good for him too because, when I am happy, I work a lot harder and my work is a lot better. When I first came to the company, I thought I would stay here for eighteen months and then move on. But, my work here has been so successful and rewarding that I feel I would be giving up a great opportunity if I left now.

Assistant to the Chairman of a major clothing company

Good Management Fosters Long-Term Thinking

Our manager gave us the right amount of autonomy with the right amount of input and support and he really kept up our team spirit. What made him such a good manager was that passing on of work and sharing of burdens was very well organized. He was a good listener and he expressed himself very clearly. He was great about

leading and giving us direction but still giving people ownership of their work. He showed us that he respected our time because he was a good planner and he delegated work efficiently. The difference between him and bad managers I have had is that he wasn't so self centered as a lot of others. That kind of management style fosters long-term thinking about the job and the company. And that is self-reinforcing. We had the most incredible, productive team this company has ever seen. All of the members of our team have since been promoted in the company. Our manager was promoted to a very senior position because the company was so pleased with the results our team produced.
Strategic planner for a major retail company

INFORMATION + THE CHANCE TO LEARN - XERS' MAXIMUM PRODUCTIVITY

Assemble Resources, Set Ground Rules And Trust Your People

My manager was very good about getting me up to speed, pointing me in the right direction, and then letting me get the job done. If I ever had questions, then I could always ask him for help. He really took the time to train me and introduced me slowly to my responsibilities. But when I was ready, he let me run with the ball. Then he gave me room to explore new areas and grow my job on my own initiative. I am opening up markets that my manager never even dreamed of. Now, he is moving up in the company and I am moving up with him.
Marketing manager at a publishing company

A MEMO TO MANAGERS OF GENERATION X

Based on my research for this book, here is a summary of recommendations for bringing out the best in Generation X.

- ABANDON THE SLACKER MYTH
- RECOGNIZE XERS' GENERATIONAL EXPECTATIONS
- DISTINGUISH BETWEEN ARROGANCE AND INDEPENDENCE
- SUPPORT XERS' QUEST FOR SELF-BASED CAREER SECURITY
- SPEND THE TIME UP FRONT THAT ALLOWS YOU TO DELEGATE
- BUILD CORPORATE CULTURES THAT VALUE THE INDIVIDUAL
- PROVIDE XERS WITH OPPORTUNITIES TO EXCEL
- GIVE XERS THE PSYCHOLOGICAL SPACE TO THRIVE
- FOCUS ON RESULTS, NOT PROCESS
- GIVE XERS RESPONSIBILITY FOR TANGIBLE END-PRODUCTS
- SET CLEAR DEADLINES FOR TANGIBLE END-PRODUCTS
- PROVIDE XERS WITH AS MUCH INFORMATION AS YOU CAN
- KEEP OPEN LINES OF COMMUNICATION
- TREAT XERS' QUESTIONS AS OPPORTUNITIES TO TEACH
- OUTLINE AND CLEARLY DEFINE GOALS
- LET XERS MANAGE AS MUCH OF OUR TIME AS POSSIBLE
- MAKE WORK A PROVING GROUND FOR XERS' CREATIVITY

- BUILD CONSTANT FEEDBACK LOOPS

- MAKE FEEDBACK ACCURATE, SPECIFIC AND TIMELY

- CELEBRATE XERS' SUCCESSES

Of course, these conclusions are drawn from interviews with a specific group of people working at a specific time. But these conclusions apply to a broad range of situations.

The main prerequisite to managing this generation—and every new generation—is to demolish preconceptions and free people to perform at their best. That's always been a goal of good management. It will still be true when Xers are the crusty old curmudgeons in the corner offices.

Good managers today will help Xers become the leaders of the next millennium.

CONCLUSION:

An Xer's Parting Observations

THE ULTIMATE LEARNING PROCESS

I started my work on this book in late 1993. With each new stage in the writing process, I have learned new lessons from the words of my interviewees, reached greater levels of understanding about this generation, and become ever more convinced that Generation X has what it takes to lead in the twenty-first century.

MANAGERS FIND TWO USEFUL CONCLUSIONS IN THIS BOOK

First, I want you to believe in Generation X. I hope you will look anew at the Xers whom you manage, maybe the Xers in your family, and others whom you know. Please, try to refocus your interpretation of their needs and expectations, their perceptions and motivations. If you can refocus your understanding through the lens of this book, you will get to know Xers for who we really are—and take the first step toward maximizing the talents of this generation.

Second, this book holds not only self-portraits of Xers but Xers' portraits of you—at your worst and at your best. Do you see yourself in this book? Think back on your interactions with Xers—maybe a few highlights and a few low points. If it is easier now to make sense of those interactions, I have done my job in this book. I hope the book sheds light on the dynamics of your management interactions with Xers and renders more clear the causal connections which influence Xers' range of responses. Use this book as a road map to reach the responses you hope to motivate in the Xers whom you manage.

XERS SHOULD FIND A TRUER SELF-PORTRAIT IN THIS BOOK

I want Xers to read this book because it holds so many self-portraits, so many common experiences. I hope that Xers who are stuck in bad management relationships will find in this book the same kind of reality check which you seek from friends over lunch and in whisper sessions behind closed doors. I hope that the success stories of self-building management relationships in this book will be a source of hope for the future.

For those Xers who are insulted by the "slacker" image promoted in the media, this book offers an alternative portrayal—Generation X according to Generation X. We can't let ourselves be defined by those who fail to understand our history and our future. This is the reality check—our future is in our own hands. By our own self-reliant creativity, we will create the economy of the future, an economy driven by new sources of value, an economy which promotes career-security from within ourselves.

HOW ONE XER TURNED FROM MANAGED TO MANAGER

While this book is written from the standpoint of the managed, my own perspective has shifted since the inception of the project. At the end of January 1994, I left the Wall Street law firm where I was working.

I left to start my own company, which is now a Connecticut corporation called Rainmaker Information Analysis & Strategic Consulting, Inc. It's a company dedicated to survey research, management consulting, and political campaign management. (I've been running political campaigns since I was 13 years old.)

Of course, I smile whenever I write about Xers' entrepreneurial nature—because I am, this moment, pursuing my own entrepreneurial dream.

In late 1994, I spent six months managing my own team of Star Xers. I wondered whether managing Xers for myself would prove to be an ironic frustration. Would I struggle with Xers like so many of the managers described by my interviewees? Would the Xers I managed whisper bad words about me at the water cooler?

The occasion was my first project with Rainmaker, the management of a State Senate campaign in Western Connecticut.

I knew that the challenge offered me the ideal proving ground for my ideas, the perfect laboratory in which to test the approach outlined in Managing Generation X. Was fate smiling on me or laughing at me? As the experience unfolded, my every expectation was exceeded and I was truly stunned by the richness of our team's performance.

My candidate was an Xer, a 29-year-old Democratic City Councilman. He was an attorney with a large family, an articulate but unseasoned candidate, a good record as a Councilman, and great potential as a future State Senator.

XER VERSUS XER IN THE POLITICAL ARENA

The problem was our opponent, also an Xer, a 30-year-old Republican State Representative, elected in 1992 with 67 percent of the vote. He had demonstrated unprecedented fund-raising ability and, even more forbidding, had achieved great notoriety by filing a lawsuit to force the State to limit government spending. On top of that, the district in which we were running was a bastion of Republican strength in a year when Republicans would ultimately achieve historic gains at the polls.

Democrats everywhere feared the wrath of angry voters eager to exact revenge on local candidates for their discontent with national Democratic leaders. It was going to be a very tough race.

The first task for any underdog in politics is to demonstrate to observers that the race is not lost before it even begins. We had to build credibility and prove that we had a chance to win. The challenge was too much to rely on the ordinary—only by the most extraordinary efforts would we be able to get in the race, much less win it. I knew that our best hope was to assemble a team of Star Xers willing to devote their talents and innovations to the campaign.

I wanted a team capable of routinely accomplishing the impossible, a team which could out-perform the best campaigns that anyone had ever seen, a team which could re-shape the entire political landscape of a community. The goal was formidable, but dictated by necessity.

How would I go about recruiting the team? Anyone who joined the team was going to have to work fifteen hours a day, seven days a week, for months on end, with no pay, and no break until the polls closed on election day.

MAKING THE NEED FOR SELF-BUILDING COUNT

I had only one form of remuneration to offer—self-building. I began to seek out Xers who might be looking for a career change, Xers who had some interest in politics or public affairs, Xers who wanted to learn the business of election campaigns, Xers whose interest in adding skills and abilities and experience to their repertoires exceeded their short-term need for money. What I found was five incredible stars, ranging in age from twenty-one to thirty, ranging in work experience from Wendy who was fresh out of college to Richard who had worked for nine years—first in advertising and then in real estate management.

The other three were in their mid-twenties—Meghan was emerging from five years in a major insurance company, Jeff had worked for five years as a computer consultant in the information industry, and Ted had worked for two years as a field organizer in a pubic affairs organization (the only one with anything resembling campaign experience on his resume).

None of them had ever worked on an election campaign, but all of them were eager to learn and ready to face the challenge ahead.

My first goal was to create a self-building environment, in which each member of the team was valuable, in which each member of the team had her own working space, in which each member of the team had access to maximal information resources, in which each member of the team had the opportunity to make meaningful contributions in the form of tangible end-results. We rented an office the size of Texas, so that each member of the team could have his or her own office.

Each member of the team was named Deputy Campaign Manager and each was given 100 percent responsibility for a particular area of the campaign—fund-raising, research & scheduling, computer database management, field organization, and field execution. Everyone had a learning curve—my door was always open and I went out of my way to provide information from every source imaginable.

In no time, everyone was expert in his or her own area. Everyone set their own goals and their own timetables, which they ran by the team in our quick morning round-table meetings. We set priorities together and we made decisions together. Individually, each member of the team defined his own problems and created her own solutions.

We worked a lot of hours, sometimes starting as early as 5:00 a.m., often working past midnight, occasionally working around the clock. We monitored our successes together by the incredible impact we were achieving. Soon our efforts earned us a proud nickname among news people and political observers—we became known as "The Victory Team."

THIS XER VICTORY TEAM CREATED INSTANT RESULTS

The results achieved by The Victory Team were mind boggling. By the first financial filing deadline in July, we had raised more money than any state senate campaign in the entire state—more than any campaign had ever raised by that date. Our operation was more developed than that of the leading Democratic candidate for governor. In the state capital, people began to say that we were doing the impossible, making an unwinnable senate race into a dead heat.

Before long, lobbyists and union leaders and senators alike began making the journey to Victory Team Headquarters to see if the rumors were true—to see if we had, indeed, put together a campaign like no one had ever seen before. Soon we became the number one priority race for the senate leadership, despite the fact that every intangible factor remained against us, that our chance for victory was still against all odds.

As the campaign progressed, we built a relative army of active volunteers. Funds continued to pour into our treasury. We received dozens and dozens of endorsements, from elected officials, police, teachers, doctors and nurses, labor unions, select business leaders, women's groups, and public affairs organizations of every sort. The Victory Team was redefining politics and the art of campaigning—everyone who visited our office exclaimed, "I have never seen anything like this."

In every area, The Victory Team found new ways to solve old problems. We did everything better—from the age-old practice of holding signs to the sophisticated techniques of tracking voters by computer. While Jeff created software which may revolutionize the technology of campaign management, Joe—another team member—suggested we don costumes for Halloween as we went through our morning rush-hour ritual of holding signs at major intersections.

Having worked in more than two dozen campaigns, I can say that I have never seen a more effective effort than that produced by The Victory Team. Our efforts led United States Senator Christopher Dodd to say in a local newspaper that we were "running the best state Senate race in Connecticut." On election day, we received 49.1 percent of the vote, leading every other candidate on the Democratic line of the ballot in our district.

In the end, 49.1 percent wasn't enough, though. The Republican won.

MOVING FROM SHORT-TERM DEFEAT TO LASTING VICTORY

Still, The Victory Team did not languish in defeat. Our candidate is still a successful lawyer in his home town. Meghan is now a professional fund-raiser in a charitable organization. Wendy and Ted went to work after the campaign for two high profile public affairs organizations. Richard is considering a run for public office himself. And Jeff is now one of my partners in Rainmaker.

My experience with The Victory Team was the final proof I needed to write the third and final draft of *Managing Generation X*—the final proof to me that maximizing the unique creative power of this generation is worth the time and energy of any manager and any institution. As my own company goes forward, we are conducting ongoing research on Generation X—with each new survey, each new focus group, each new in-depth interview, I know that every Xer can be a Star and every Xer team can be a Victory Team.

Index

Managing Generation X™

Bringing Out the Best in Young Talent

Results Aimed At Your Bottom Line

Bruce Tulgan is the founder of **Rainmaker, Inc.**, a strategic think tank for hire. The other managing principals of Rainmaker are Jeff Coombs and Jeff Katz. Coombs, a veteran of the information systems industry, is Rainmaker's computer wizard. Katz, who served as a Foreign Service Officer in Southeast Asia, is Rainmaker's expert in strategic dynamics.

Please send me information about . . .

☐ Scheduling Bruce Tulgan for speaking engagements

☐ Rainmaker's Target Generation X Research

☐ Rainmakers's Managing Generation X On-Site Consulting Programs

☐ Rainmaker, Inc.

Name _____

Address _____

Phone _____

E-Mail _____

Fax _____

BUSINESS REPLY CARD

FIRST-CLASS MAIL   PERMIT NO. 535   NEW HAVEN CT

POSTAGE WILL BE PAID BY ADDRESSEE

RAINMAKER, INC.

53 LAWRENCE STREET SUITE ONE

NEW HAVEN CT 06511

BUSINESS REPLY CARD

FIRST-CLASS MAIL   PERMIT NO. 243   SANTA MONICA CA

POSTAGE WILL BE PAID BY ADDRESSEE

MERRITT PUBLISHING

POST OFFICE BOX 955

SANTA MONICA CA 90406-9875

SWAK